KEEPERS OF THE VINEYARD

The Puritan Ministry and Collective Culture in Colonial New England

George Selement

**UNIVERSITY
PRESS OF
AMERICA**

LANHAM • NEW YORK • LONDON

Copyright © 1984 by

University Press of America,™ Inc.

4720 Boston Way
Lanham, MD 20706

3 Henrietta Street
London WC2E 8LU England

ISBN (Perfect): 0-8191-3877-0
ISBN   (Cloth): 0-8191-3876-2

All University Press of America books are produced on acid-free
paper which exceeds the minimum standards set by the National
Historical Publications and Records Commission.

To Darrett B. Rutman

Contents

Chapter One

Historians and Collective Culture

With roughly 225 books and 800 articles published on American Puritanism since Perry Miller wrote The New England Mind: The Seventeenth Century in 1939, why add another? "It could in fact be argued," as Edmund S. Morgan quipped in 1966, "that we already know more about the Puritans than sane men should want to know, that we ought therefore to declare a moratorium on further investigation and turn our attention to less familiar fields." But as Morgan also recognized "rewards often increase instead of diminishing as investigation spreads and deepens," and his observation especially applies to the pastoral work of Puritan divines. This aspect of their ministry was as vital as preaching; yet, historians have written "one hundred pages describing the clerical thought in published treatises and occasional unpublished manuscripts for every two or three pages about pastoral work." More than filling an informational gap about the cure of souls, however, an investigation of this long-neglected topic reveals much about historiographical issues central to Puritan studies: How scholarly were Puritan divines? Was there an ideological and social gap between ministers and laymen? Did collective mentality prevail in New England? Did Puritan treatises reflect such a mentality? Were the Puritans tribal? Did they fear death? How and when did New England change from a Puritan to Yankee society?[1]

To explain fully all the ramifications of these historiographical concerns would require a book-length monograph or two, but selective elaboration is in order as a context for what the pastoral labors of Puritan ministers can reveal about such questions. The link between each of these issues is the degree to which New England society was Puritan. As Robert Allen Skotheim explained almost twenty years ago, historians have been trying to determine how much Puritanism influenced New Englanders since before the turn of the twentieth century. The histories of Moses Coit Tyler and Edward Eggleston, Skotheim found, "foreshadowed two divergent tendencies in the writing of many major American histories of ideas during the XXth century." Tyler's A History of American Literature, 1607-1765 (1878) provided a model for those scholars who would see New England as a "thinking community" best described through its ministerial literature. Intellectual clergymen, therefore, were the region's prime movers, disseminating ideas that captivated the masses and established a unified Puritan New England. Moreover, Tyler admired this Puritan era as a "wonderful epoch."[2]

In contrast, Eggleston in The Transit of Civilization (1900) played down the influence of elite ministers and emphasized the role of a "popular mind" brought to America as cultural baggage from England. "From the English spoken in the days of the Stuart kings," Eggleston wrote, "came our primitive speech, and the opinions, prejudices, and modes of thinking of the English in that day lay at the bottom of what intellectual life there was in the colonies." Furthermore, New Englanders had "no considerable part in the higher intellectual life of the age; the great artistic passions of Shakespeare and Milton touched them not at any point." Rather their "characteristics, long since lost or obscured in England, may yet be recognized in the folk-lore and folk-speech, the superstitions and beliefs of people in America." Thus, for Eggleston, New England was not Puritan but pluralistic, and his sympathies were not with Puritanism's "false and harsh ideals" but with the popular mind where there were opportunities for "progress" and "enlightenment."[3]

Because Progressive historians, who saw Puritanism as an enemy of modernization, dominated the profession in the first decades of the twentieth century, Eggleston's paradigm overshadowed Tyler's interpretation. Skotheim rightly pointed to Vernon Louis Parrington's Main Currents in American Thought (1927), the "most preferred" American history published between 1920 and 1935, as a solid example of Eggleston's influence. An even better one, however, is James Truslow Adams who in The Founding of New England (1921) asserted that "the Puritan element, in the sense of New England church membership, amounted to only about four thousand persons out of about sixty-five thousand." The masses, he concluded, had migrated for land "to better their condition." To be sure, ministers and magistrates were Puritan, "even inflicting torture and taking human life to maintain their position." But these Puritan bigots were not the real founders of America. The true Americans were those who defeated the theocrats:

2

"the leaders and citizens of Rhode Island, the mar-
tyred Quakers, and the men and women of Massachusetts
and the other colonies, who so lived and wrought and
died that the glory of an heritage of intellectual
freedom might be ours, are the Americans whom . . .
it should be our duty to honor." For Adams, then,
ministers and their oppressive theology did not
represent New England--let alone America; they, their
dry sermons, and Puritanism, an "indelible stain on
the pages of American history," were best forgotten.[4]

Progressive interpretations, though dominant,
were not unchallenged. As early as 1925, Kenneth
Ballard Murdock demonstrated that Increase Mather, a
Boston preacher, was neither a bigot nor unrepresenta-
tive of New Englanders; instead he had been the "un-
questioned leader of his people for more than half a
century, always in church, often in politics, and in-
variably in those human affairs where the example of
a strong and active life can be made to count." In
Builders of the Bay Colony (1930) Samuel Eliot Morison
proved that Mather was no exception, sketching the
lives of other likeable Puritans in leadership roles.
Moreover, Morison in a direct attack on Adams made a
strong case that "the settlers of New England were
predominantly puritan." Subsequently, Morison
strengthened his interpretations in The Founding of
Harvard College (1935), Harvard College in the Seventeenth Century (1936), and The Puritan Pronaos (1936),
all revealing a "strong Tyler-like sympathy and ad-
miration for Puritanism." Likewise, Clifford K.
Shipton made a plea for Puritanism in 1935, positing
that "there were no general anticlerical feelings in
the Puritan colonies" and deeming the ministers
"leaders in every field of intellectual advance in
New England." More importantly, two years earlier
Shipton had published his first volume of Sibley's
Harvard Graduates, a series in which he humanized the
Puritans. Believing that Murdock, Morison, and
Shipton had proven their points, Perry Miller, who
like Tyler concluded that "the mind of man is the
basic factor in human history," set out to document
that "Puritanism was one of the major expressions of
the Western intellect, that it achieved an organized
synthesis of concepts which are fundamental to our
culture, and that therefore it calls for the most
serious examination." In Orthodoxy in Massachusetts
(1933), The Puritans (1938), which he co-edited with
Thomas J. Johnson, and especially The New England
Mind: The Seventeenth Century (1939) Miller

3

accomplished his goal. A few years later Edmund S. Morgan finished off whatever remained of Progressive orthodoxy by showing that Puritans were humanistic in their sexual attitudes--an area in which everyone thought the Puritans benighted--and family lives.[5]

By 1945, therefore, these five scholars had demolished the Progressive paradigm, erecting a new model that portrayed New England as a thinking community led by intellectual ministers. Puritan New England, meaning a region unified in its commitment to Puritan ideas, became a shibboleth in New England studies, as historians sought "the innermost propulsion of the United States" in the ideas to be found in clerical documents. True, a skeptic or two remained. In an otherwise favorable review of The New England Mind, Odell Shepard reminded scholars that, as Eggleston had argued, the New England mind was "already shaped to the pattern of English town and village communities before it tried, with amazing success, to transport that pattern across the sea." And Thomas Jefferson Wertenbaker wrote The Puritan Oligarchy: The Founding of American Civilization (1947) as if the Harvard Revisionists, as these scholars came to be called, had never written. But most professionals concurred with Carl Bridenbaugh's 1940 declaration that "as the Bible was the ultimate authority of the Puritans, so The New England Mind must be a Sibylline Book for students of American history, literature, and thought.[6]

The late 1940's and the 1950's bore out Bridenbaugh's prediction. The ongoing publications of Murdock, Morison, Shipton, Miller, and Morgan obviously promoted that end. Though Shipton's biographies chiefly humanized the Puritans, he focused on ministerial ideas whenever possible. Similarly, Morison explored social more than intellectual history but was sympathetic to the latter. Murdock, Miller, and Morgan, however, feverishly wrote and promoted intellectual history. Murdock's Literature & Theology in Colonial New England (1949) declared that "the intellectual life of the New England colonies was dominated by Puritan thought" and left traces of Puritanism in the American character. Miller's The New England Mind: From Colony to Province (1953), Roger Williams: His Contribution to the American Tradition (1953), and Errand into the Wilderness (1956), all reinforced Murdock's conclusion.

So too did Morgan's The Puritan Dilemma: The Story
of John Winthrop (1958).[7]

   Equally important were the publications of other
scholars who adopted the methodology, though not all
the interpretations, of the Harvard Revisionists.
Several biographers emphasized the humanistic and in-
tellectual lives of Puritan leaders: Bradford Smith,
Bradford of Plymouth (1951); George Allen Cook, John
Wise: Early American Democrat (1952); Otho T. Beall,
Jr.,and Richard H. Shryock, Cotton Mather: First
Significant Figure in American Medicine (1954);
Raymond P. Stearns, The Strenuous Puritan: Hugh
Peter, 1598-1660 (1954); and Ola Elizabeth Winslow,
Master Roger Williams, A Biography (1957).   Walter S.
Ong carried on Miller's investigation of Ramist logic
in Ramus: Method and the Decay of Dialogue: From
the Art of Discourse to the Art of Reason (1958).
Following Morison's interest in Puritans and Indians,
Douglas Edward Leach painted a sympathetic picture of
the Puritan role in King Philip's War, declaring at
one point in Flintlock and Tomahawk that "the New
England Indians were a primitive people, occupying a
much lower level of civilization than that of the
English settlers."   Even Alan Simpson's Puritanism in
Old and New England (1955), a work that defined Puritanism differently than Miller, relied on literary
sources.   In addition to these monographs, editors
published seven volumes of Puritan documents, exploring various aspects of Puritan intellectual life, and
over 100 journal articles sprang from issues raised
by the Harvard Revisionists.[8]

   Even the work of social historians--some of whom
thought the Revisionists were overemphasizing the
"literary evidences of Puritan thinkers"--dovetailed
with intellectual history. Winslow's Meetinghouse
Hill 1630-1783 (1952) described the "typical procedures" of churches "in relation to various aspects of
community life," a topic Miller "was simply not interested in." Similarly, Emil Oberholzer, Jr.'s
Delinquent Saints mined church records to determine
the disciplinary actions of New England churches but
still defined Puritanism in Revisionist terms and saw,
like Winslow, his work as simply an "attempt to study"
an unexplored area. Even Bernard Bailyn, the most
outspoken critic of Miller in the 1950's, wrote The
New England Merchants in the Seventeenth Century
(1955) to construct an "account of the growth of the
forces in New England society that worked in

opposition to the old Puritanism" rather than contra-
dict Miller's formulations in The New England Mind:
From Colony to Province. In fact, Bailyn deemed that
volume "an impressive, original interpretation of one
of the important transitions in American history."9

By 1960, thirty years of Puritan studies had
created a productive synthesis, one that portrayed
New England as shaped by humanistic Puritans who
lived in a thinking community led by intellectual
ministers. In contrast, the next ten years wrought
a split--one reminiscent of the Tyler-Eggleston
dichotomy--among scholars. Most specialists continued publishing in the Revisionist vein. This
group, and by far the largest and most influential,
published three readers, eighteen biographies,
twenty-three edited volumes, thirty topical studies,
and about 175 articles by the end of 1970. This
prolific avalanche enabled Morgan to declare by 1966
that New England historiography had reached "a level
of sophistication unmatched in the study of any other
part of American history." Often these writers gen-
tly amended the interpretations of Miller, who died
in 1963. Indeed, Michael McGiffert in 1970 published
an insightful article sorting out the interpretative
differences between forty-six historians studying
seventeenth-century New England, and there may have
been as many as eighty scholars writing at the time.
But the authors of the above 250 publications subscribed to Miller's methodology of writing New
England history on the basis of literary sources
written by elite ministers. As McGiffert put it in
1972, Miller's The New England Mind remained "the
monumental study to which all subsequent work on the
subject is elaboration, clarification, qualification,
or contradiction." Thus, Puritan scholars had
arrived, via Miller, to Tyler's position: there was
a Puritan New England.10

Meanwhile, a coterie of historians--McGiffert
named eleven leaders in 1970--had been raising doubts
about the existence of "an entity that can properly
be called Puritan New England." Like Eggleston, they
traced New England life to Old World traditions.
Sumner Chilton Powell in Puritan Village (1963) wrote
about life at Sudbury, Massachusetts,with--despite
its title--little reference to Puritanism, explaining
agricultural, social, political, and economic practices in terms of their English cultural origins and
adaptations to the New World environment. Moreover,

Powell relied on non-literary sources, like town and
court records, rather than sermons. Darrett B.
Rutman, unlike Powell who never mentioned his differences with the Revisionists, openly attacked Miller
for violating "sound historical method" and declared
Morgan's interpretations were "open to serious question." Especially troublesome, given the battle
Revisionists had fought with Progressives, was Rutman's argument that ministers were "isolated from
reality" and published books that had little to do
with understanding the actuality of the "man in the
village lane." To comprehend New England society,
Rutman turned to town, colony, court, and other non-
literary sources and from that basis in Winthrop's
Boston declared: "Indeed, the adjective 'Puritan,'
together with the arguments surrounding it, have
seemed inapplicable to Boston in any meaningful way,
the total community being fragmented from almost the
very beginning and, being made up of ordinary people."
Likewise, Philip J. Greven, Jr., reported that social
historians rested their work "upon the soundest basis
possible--not upon literary evidence, which too often
has proven unreliable and misleading, but upon solid
demographic evidence." Armed with the methods of
aggregative analysis, family reconstitution, and
quantification, this new generation of historians
published a nucleus of articles in the 1960's in a
spirit, as McGiffert judged, "inclined to be exclama-
tory in celebrating their liberation from the 'Millerite Establishment' and their own rising empire."
In 1970 John Demos's A Little Commonwealth: Family
Life in Plymouth Colony, Greven's Four Generations:
Population, Land, and Family in Colonial Andover,
Massachusetts, and Kenneth A. Lockridge's A New
England Town, The First Hundred Years: Dedham, Massachusetts, 1636-1736 climaxed a decade of innovation,
inspiring one reviewer to conclude: "The New World
has been slow to acquire the Old World's sophisti-
cated techniques of social history. Perhaps it can
atone for its tardiness through the comparative data
it alone can supply."[11]

     The historiography of early New England has be-
come increasingly complex from 1970 to date. To be
sure, many scholars have remained steadfast in their
respective methodological camps. Intellectual his-
torians--still the dominant group--have published
about 95% of the six readers, fifteen biographies,
seventeen edited volumes, forty-six topical studies,
and 434 articles that have appeared in the field

since 1970, varying little in their work from the methodology of the Revisionists. The five books and eight articles of Sacvan Bercovitch are a prime example. Despite their brilliance and revisionary interpretations, Bercovitch relied exclusively on literary evidence. Likewise, most social historians "persist in ignoring ideas," especially those to be found in sermons. Lockridge's Literacy in Colonial New England: An Inquiry into the Social Context of Literacy in the Early Modern West (1974) is filled with graphs, tables, and statistics and striking in its avoidance of literary evidence. Even his footnotes-- primarily statistical clarifications--fail to recognize the contribution of intellectual historians. Similarly, Jon Butler, though he quoted literary scholars in his recent article on early American religion, repudiated their work by exhorting historians to understand the "marrow of American religious life" by moving "beyond the study of ecclesiology, theology, and the ministry to recover noninstitutional religious practices." Even Richard P. Gildrie's Salem, Massachusetts, 1626-1683, A Covenant Community (1975), a town study that incorporates some Revisionist interpretations, demonstrates that the concerns and methods of social historians remain largely outside the "Millerite framework."[12]

A minority of scholars, however, have used an eclectic methodology to profit from the approaches of both social and intellectual historians. Rutman led the way in American Puritanism: Faith and Practice (1970). Attempting "to bridge the gap between these schools," he developed a paradigm involving the impact of both ministerial thought and English traditions on New England society. Four years later, Paul Boyer and Stephen Nissenbaum published an excellent analysis of Salem witchcraft using the sources and procedures of literary and demographic scholars. In 1975 Emery Elliott's Power and the Pulpit in Puritan New England combined the insights of Demos, Greven, Lockridge, Powell, and Rutman with those of Miller, Morgan, Norman Petit, James Jones, and Bercovitch, as well as borrowing theoretical models from social scientists like Erik Erikson, to achieve a multi-dimensioned account of seventeenth-century New England. Most recently, Greven moved beyond his pure demography in Four Generations to an interdisciplinary understanding of early American society in The Protestant Temperament: Patterns of Child-Rearing, Religious Experience, and the Self in

<u>Early America</u> (1977). The writings of these and other
innovators, and the sheer bulk of publications since
1970, has certainly enriched Puritan studies but so
complicated matters that no scholar has undertaken
even surveying the field in McGiffert fashion. Indeed, one capable specialist thinks the only way to
get a "handle" on the materials is to write "a series
of essays pulling together disparate sources on particular topics" rather than any "efforts at comprehen-
siveness."[13]

It is, then, these historiographical issues--
first raised by Tyler and Eggleston and then immensely
complicated by the myriad publications of the last
eighty years--that <u>Keepers of the Vineyard</u> addresses.
Using the little-known pastoral work of the Puritan
clergy as a vehicle, it is possible to determine the
amount of daily interaction between ministers and
ordinary people, and such contact is crucial for
assessing how much Puritanism ministers embedded in
seventeenth-century New England. Their routine
labors also reveal whether pastors were evangelical
in their outreach to all New Englanders or tribally
focused on church members, another critical deter-
minant for the existence of a Puritan New England.
Moreover, the way in which preachers disseminated
their pamphlets reveals the amount of influence
Puritan literature had on New England traditions.
And finally pastoral duties yield much insight to the
pace of secularization in the region, documenting how
rapidly New Englanders shifted their allegiance from
Puritan ideals to the Yankee values salient in the
American Revolution. In sum, mundane pastoral work
indicates much about the "formulas, the assumptions,
that comprise collective mentality in seventeenth-
century New England." Proper handling of such data
may also further "bridge the gap" between social and
intellectual historians, as suggested by J. William
T. Youngs, Jr.: "The pastoral character of the Puritan ministry, the nature of the print marketplace,
and the dissemination of Christian doctrine to native
Americans all testify to the capacity of Puritanism
to circulate well beyond the confines of a clerical
elite."[14]

1. Morgan, "The Historians of Early New England," in
Ray Allen Billington, ed., The Reinterpretation
of Early American History: Essays in Honor of
John Edwin Pomfret (New York: W. W. Norton edition,
1968), 41-42; George Selement, "Publication and
the Puritan Minister," William and Mary Quarterly,
3d Ser., XXXVII (1980), 221.

2. Skotheim, "The Writing of American Histories of
Ideas: Two Traditions in the XXth Century,"
Journal of the History of Ideas, XXV (1964), 257.

3. Ibid., 259-260; Eggleston, The Transit of Civilization: From England to America in the Seventeenth Century (Boston: Beacon edition, 1959),
1-3.

4. Skotheim, "The Writing of American Histories of
Ideas," 268; Adams, The Founding of New England
(Boston, 1921), 121-122, 276-277.

5. Murdock, Increase Mather: The Foremost Puritan
(Cambridge, Mass., 1925), 391; Morison, Builders
of the Bay Colony (Boston, 1930), 343; Skotheim,
"The Writing of American Histories of Ideas,"
272, 274; Shipton, "A Plea for Puritanism," Amer-
ican Historical Review, XL (1935), 467; Morgan,
"The Puritans and Sex," New England Quarterly, XV
(1942), 591-607; and The Puritan Family: Religion
& Domestic Relations in Seventeenth-Century New
England (Boston, 1944).

6. Miller, Errand into the Wilderness (New York:
Harper Torchbooks edition, 1964), viii; Shepard's
review of Miller's The New England Mind: The
Seventeenth Century (Cambridge, Mass., 1939) is
in The New York Times Book Review (December 17,
1939), 9, and Bridenbaugh's is in American Historical Review, XLV (1939-1940), 889.

7. Murdock, Literature & Theology in Colonial New
England (Cambridge, Mass., 1949), 173.

8. Leach, Flintlock and Tomahawk: New England in
King Philip's War (New York, 1958), 6. This
and subsequent estimates about the number of
publications on the Puritans are based on a
bibliography I have compiled.

9. Bernard Bailyn's review of Perry Miller, The New England Mind: From Colony to Province (Cambridge, Mass., 1953) in New England Quarterly, XXVII (1954), 116-118; Ola Elizabeth Winslow, Meetinghouse Hill 1630-1783 (New York, 1952), vii; Morgan, "The Historians of Early New England," 55; Oberholzer, Delinquent Saints: Disciplinary Action in the Early Congregational Churches of Massachusetts (New York, 1956), 3.

10. Morgan, "The Historians of Early New England," 41; McGiffert, "American Puritan Studies in the 1960's," William and Mary Quarterly, 3d Ser., XXVII (1970), 37-38; McGiffert, ed., God's Plot: The Paradoxes of Puritan Piety, Being the Autobiography & Journal of Thomas Shepard (Amherst, Mass., 1972), 240.

11. McGiffert, "American Puritan Studies in the 1960's," 58-60; Rutman, Winthrop's Boston: Portrait of a Puritan Town, 1630-1649 (Chapel Hill, 1965), 284, viii-ix; Rutman, "God's Bridge Falling Down: 'Another Approach' to New England Puritanism Assayed," William and Mary Quarterly, 3d Ser., XIX (1962), 409; Rutman, "The Mirror of Puritan Authority" in McGiffert, ed., Puritanism and the American Experience (Reading, Mass., 1969), 78; Greven, "Historical Demography and Colonial America," William and Mary Quarterly, 3d Ser., XXIV (1967), 450; review essay by John M. Murrin in History and Theory: Studies in the Philosophy of History, XI (1972), 275.

12. Rutman to Selement, November 12, 1981; Butler, "Magic, Astrology, and the Early American Religious Heritage, 1600-1760," American Historical Review, LXXXIV (1979), 317-318; Rutman, American Puritanism: Faith and Practice (New York, 1970), 132.

13. Rutman, American Puritanism, vi; Boyer and Nissenbaum, Salem Possessed: The Social Origins of Witchcraft (Cambridge, Mass., 1974), passim; J. William T. Youngs, Jr., to Selement, January 23, 1982.

14. David D. Hall, "The World of Print and Collective Mentality in Seventeenth-Century New England," in John Higham and Paul K. Conkin, eds., New Directions in American Intellectual History

(Baltimore, 1979), 177; Youngs, "Perry Miller and the 'Buzzing Factuality' of Colonial New England," paper read before the meeting of the American Historical Association, Washington, D.C., December 29, 1980, p. 15.

Chapter Two

The Faithful Shepherd

One of the main reasons historians have debated
the existence of a Puritan New England stems from
their view of the ministry. Revisionists like Miller
portrayed Puritan divines as sacrificing "their health
to the production of massive tomes" and counting "that
day lost in which they did not spend ten or twelve
hours in their studies." For Revisionists, however,
such scholarly habits did not isolate clergymen from
laity because "Puritan ideas were something more than
the subject of a discourse among intellectuals . . .
they reflected the cares of the society as a whole."
Morgan even believed, and apparently still holds, that
commoners "had no ideas of their own" and thus had to
embrace ministerial thought, a process which established collective culture in a Puritan New England.
Social historians also accepted that preachers were
intellectuals but, rediscovering the non-ideological
traditions from England that shaped New England
society, divorced the everyday life of commoners from
the clerical world of ideas and publications. Rutman's perspective in "The Mirror of Puritan Authority"
was typical: "The historian must, of course, address
himself to the problem of New England's intellectuals.
Isolated from reality as they were, they clung for
almost half a century to ideals which grew more outdated with the passing of each day, and then gradually
and subtly accommodated their ideals to the realities
of the situation facing them." Though five years
later Rutman in American Puritanism gave more credit
to the impact of ministerial thought, other social
historians continue to argue colonists "proved sur-
prisingly ignorant of elemental Christian beliefs
and practices" that occupied ivory-tower ministers.
Most social historians, therefore, continue to find
"Miller's noetic concerns largely irrelevant," clergymen to be isolated thinkers, and like Eggleston the
origins of early American society in the folk traditions of "early modern Europe, especially of England."
Thus, for demographers, there is no Puritan New England.[1]

If one quoted Puritan hagiography and ministerial
diaries selectively, this consensus about the "intellectual muscularity" of the clergy would be affirmed.
The famous John Cotton allegedly would have preferred

to give his callers "an handful of Money" than have
his studies interrupted. Another account has Richard
Mather of Dorchester, who from his youth had been a
"hard student," persuading friends to drag him from
his deathbed into his study, declaring in its doorway,
unable to proceed: "Is it not a lamentable thing that
I should lose so much time?" Following in his father's footsteps, Increase Mather claimed he spent
"seldom less than 16 hours in 24" in his study, and
his son, Cotton, outstripped them all by publishing
388 books, composing a plethora of manuscripts, and
fasting in his study at least 450 days over his long
career. The physical toll of such feats prompted
Israel Loring, a Sudbury preacher, to conclude that
the studious life of sedentary ministers "oftimes
spoils their digestion, ruins the good Temperament of
the Blood, and fills them with Infirmities." Loring
might have cited Thomas Parker as an example, for
Cotton Mather reported that the "immoderate Studies"
of the Newbury divine caused one of his eyes to swell
"until it came out of his Head." But before agreeing
with the native Americans at New Haven that, like John
Davenport, every minister was a "So Big Study Man,"
it is imperative to recognize that Puritan biographers,
eulogists, and diarists often inflated their stories
for didactic purposes. Cotton Mather, who published
a book on medical cures, surely knew that Parker's
eyes were diseased but exaggerated his studiousness
to inspire readers of the Magnalia to erudition and
respect for the clergy. To be sure, preachers spent
more time in their libraries than anyone else--except
perhaps for their peers at Harvard--and to that extent were the intellectuals of New England, but the
twelve-hour days of studying that hagiographers popularized are myths.[2]

Take hagiography again. In one funeral sermon
Benjamin Colman, author of eighty-four publications,
remarked that Increase "lov'd his Study to a kind of
excess," and if the prolific Colman thought Mather
extreme, surely most clergymen, who never published
even one tract, would have agreed. An eulogy on
Thomas Shepard, Jr., who died from smallpox that he
contracted while visiting his Charlestown parishioners,
itemized the "Variety" of ministerial labors performed
by the typical Puritan divine, praising him as the
poor man's friend, the blind man's eyes, the "wandring
wildred Soul's Conductor Wise," the widow's solace,
the orphan's father, and the sick man's visitant."
Another on Michael Wigglesworth--now remembered for

his Day of Doom and for sitting in his study fretting
over whether or not to tell his neighbor that his
"dores blow to and fro with the wind in some danger
to break"--praised him for years of active service at
Malden: "Visiting and comforting the Afflicted; Encouraging the Private Meetings; Catechizing the Children of the Flock; and managing the Government of the
Church; and attending the Sick, not only in his own
Town, but also in all those of the Vicinity. Thus he
did, unto the last." Likewise, Jonathan Mitchel,
whose "chief Labors" supposedly were in his Cambridge
study and pulpit, received praise for visiting "his
Flock; not upon Trivial Designs, but with serious and
solemn addresses to their Souls." Such accounts, and
they are myriad, also overstate the case, for no
human being can be all things to all men. But, as
with ministerial scholarship, they reflect a kernel
of truth--uncultivated by historians--namely, that
Puritan divines lived close to their people, not in
an ivory tower.[3]

Evidence in diaries, letters, and solid histories
like Winthrop's Journal confirm that pastors--even
those like Increase and Cotton Mather--were abroad in
their communities, involving themselves in every
aspect of New England life. Combining these sources
with Puritan hagiography, and keeping in mind that
especially the latter exaggerates but nonetheless
represents the past, it is possible to document the
extent to which pastors personally led parishioners
to grace, comforted the afflicted, helped the sick,
aided the needy, and reproved sinners. In short, how
much were ministers walled up in their libraries
writing tomes and preparing sermons as compared to
catering to the everyday needs of laymen? Did clergymen interact enough with commoners to establish and
share a collective mentality?

Beginning with the non-sermonic ways that ministers imparted theology to the laity, clearly pastors
were often in the homes of New Englanders, as well
as counseling them at the parsonage study. Of course,
there were individual differences between ministers
--one might like visiting more than another and thus
do more of it. For instance, when Increase Mather
called on "10 sick Families" in a single day, he re-
gretted being pulled from his study which made his
words "Few . . . Pertinent and Ponderous, and Forc-
ible." In contrast, John Hancock of Lexington published little but scattered "the Clouds of Melancholy

that hung upon People's Spirits." The gregarious
preacher even liked to joke on pastoral visits, as
when during lunch with a wealthy parishioner he "put
his knife on the cheese, first this way and then that,
as if in doubt where to begin. 'Where shall I cut
this cheese, Mrs. Smith?' he asked. 'Cut it where
you have a mind to Mr. Hancock,' was the answer.
'Then,' said he, 'I think I will cut it at home.'"
However, as Miller wrote about the New England mind,
it makes little difference whether I draw an anecdote about Thomas Shepard's catechizing or Cotton
Mather's, for within certain bounds they shared common methodologies. And to describe every methodological nuance and personality difference between
ministers is a crashing bore. The subsequent description, therefore, provides representative examples to illustrate the wide range of theological
counseling done by pastors, to show how it must have
sapped vast amounts of time from their sermon prepara-
tion (let alone scholarly work), and to measure the
degree of collective mentality in early New England.[4]

Puritan divines began working with New Englanders
as children. Ezekiel Rogers of Rowley called a dozen
or so to his home on certain evenings, and "one by
one, he would examine them, How they walked with God?
How they spent their time? What good Books they read?
Whether they pray'd without ceasing? And he would
therewithal admonish them to take heed of such Tempta-
tions and Corruptions, as he thought most endangered
them." Then there was the "noble exercise" of catechizing whereby "thousands, thousands!," wrote Cotton
Mather, "have blessed God, with wonders and praises,
for the good success of it." This involved ministers
either inviting "Young People to their Houses, num-
bring and sorting of them as they think fit" or,
opting for the "Pauline way," going from house to
house "to treat each Person particularly about their
Everlasting Interests," or meeting the youngsters at
the church. Grindall Rawson divided Mendon into five
regions, and every Friday he held "a Meeting in One
or Other of them, where he Preached a Sermon; and
Catechised the Children which belonged unto the Families there-abouts." As children reached their "years
of discretion," pastors took them aside and with an
elder of the church examined them "touching their
knowledge of the doctrine of faith, touching their
experiences." In 1663 John Fiske recorded the differing levels of spiritual maturity among Chelmsford
youngsters. He judged Jonathan Bates "very ignorant,"

16

Benjamin Spalding's memory "better than his understanding," Olive Farwel "merely . . . understanding,"
Nathaniel Butterfield "beyond expectation as to understanding, though short of what is required," Moses
Fiske "competent touching experience," and Jonathan
Wright to have "a good relation of a work of grace,
only not clear as to the work of closure with Christ."
Fiske wanted to bring all such children of the covenant, when sixteen years and older, to where it could
be said of them, as he said of his daughter: "Sarah
Fiske upon satisfaction given to the church touching
her knowledge of the principles of faith and the work
of grace upon her soul . . . was received into full
communion and covenant with this church."[5]

   Given the complexity of the morphology of conversion, as described by Norman Pettit in The Heart Prepared: Grace and Conversion in Puritan Spiritual Life
(1966), one can easily imagine the practical difficulties of getting a townfull of young adults from ig-
norance to a good relation of grace. Sermons were a
mainstay, but ministers also had to talk with each
person, answering questions, correcting misunderstand-
ings, and quieting "Divine Terrors . . . about the
wellfare of their Precious Immortal Souls." Betty
Sewall, Judge Sewall's teenager, is a good example.
While passing the time in her father's library one
winter day in 1696, she read a sermon by John Norton
on John 7:34 and 8:21, which warned respectively:
"Ye shall seek and shall not find me," and "Ye shall
seek me and die in your sins." According to her father,
these words "ran in her mind, and terrified her
greatly." A week later Betty's fears increased when
she read in one of Cotton Mather's pamphlets: "Why
hath Satan filled thy heart?" Finally, on the following day a "little after dinner she burst out into an
amazing cry, which caus'd all the family to cry too."
Her mother, Hannah, learning that Betty "was afraid
she should goe to Hell, her Sins were not pardon'd,"
asked her if she had prayed for deliverance, but Betty
said she "feared her prayers were not heard because
her Sins not pardon'd." Although Hannah had already
sent for Samuel Willard that afternoon, when Betty had
first "given some signs of dejection and sorrow," the
busy South Church pastor did not arrive until that
evening because he had not been told of the message
earlier. As to what he said to the distressed youth,
Sewall merely recorded that Willard "discoursed with
Betty" and "pray'd excellently." Apparently, his
counsel relieved the teenager, for in a few years she

17

married Grove Hirst, a successful merchant, took her place in Boston society, and raised six children.[6]

More is known of how Thomas Shepard, the renowned "Converter of Souls" at Cambridge, dealt with John Collins, a troubled adolescent of the 1640's. Hearing that Collins deemed himself cursed under the law and the covenant and feared "death spiritual everlasting," Shepard sent for the young Harvard student. "He advised me," Collins later recounted before the Cambridge congregation, "to be constant in private prayer and to lay down at God's feet that he might do with me as he would." Though somewhat comforted by Shepard's counsel, Collins soon afterwards "lay sore wounded" with a physical injury and a deep conviction of his "vileness." Shepard again called on the now bedridden youth. After fervently praying and "wrestling" with God for the young man's life, Shepard then urged Collins "to wait on God and to part with every sin to resolve again constantly to follow God and to seek him." Thus, Shepard helped Collins overcome his fears of damnation in those two sessions by exhorting him to contrition and humiliation, the basic preparatory steps in closing with Christ. Nonetheless, Collins continued to anguish over his salvation after recuperating, as when he heard the sermons of President Dunster at Harvard and those of Jonathan Mitchell, Shepard's successor. Soon after his graduation in 1649, however, Collins joined the Cambridge church, proclaiming that he was "enwrapt" in a covenant of grace.[7]

As with Sewall and Collins, when ministers helped people surmount their emotions and prepare for grace, they still had to deal with them individually about church membership. From Pope's The Half-Way Covenant: Church Membership in Puritan New England (1969) we know the many ideological measures that preachers devised to bring laymen into the flock. But what remains unknown is how many hours ministers spent explaining innovative polity to indifferent, puzzled, or often suspicious individuals. It certainly was no easy task to change the minds of hidebound laymen; the vigilant Judge Sewall, for one, chided Benjamin Colman, who adopted Presbyterian polity in his Manifesto Church on Brattle Street, about "the 3^d Article in the Manifesto, that had shew'd no more Respect to N. E. Churches." Even when polity was not an issue, clergymen devoted much time to coaxing the overly-scrupulous and prodding the apathetic into church

membership Peter Thacher of Milton engaged one pro-
crastinator, his neighbor Sergeant Vose, in "much
serious discourse . . . about his not joining the
Church." Cotton Mather kept a catalogue of "such as
may be hopefully prepared for the Communion of the
Church," resolving that "they must be severally called
upon." He gave an entire day to landing Daniel Royce
of Boston, praying and fasting with him, sharing "a
Varitie of Discourses upon Divine Matters," and, having "drawn up in Writing, a solemn Covenant," pres-
suring the young man "until his conquered Heart and
Hand, most affectionately subscribed it, and so . . .
bound himself unto the service of the Lord." Three
pastors worked for over two months with Samuel Sewall,
who was worried over "unfitness and want of Grace,"
before he joined the South Church.[8]

It might seem that after all this training, even-
tuating in church membership, ministers would not be
bothered with further theological instruction, save
through sermons. Actually, such counseling often increased because, as Cotton Mather remarked: "Tho'
Satan can't bring a Child of God to Hell, he may
bring Hell to a Child of God." Sewall, for example,
became "more afraid" and could "hardly sit down to
the Lord's Table" because of his doubts over the
historicity of Christ. Over the years numerous
clergymen spoke with Sewall about such fears and other
theological questions--glimpses of which are scattered throughout his chatty diary. In contrast, a
little apocalyptic knowledge troubled the maid of
Ebenezer Pemberton, minister of the Old South Church
of Boston. When the blacksmith shop of Joseph Hubbard
and a "Boat-builder's Shed" burnt in 1708, she saw
the "Light of the Fire reflecting from a Black Cloud,
and came crying" to Pemberton "under Consternation;
supposing the last Conflagration had begun." Less
scrupulous parishioners needed just as much personal
attention. Cotton Mather visited six to eight families a week to make them orthodox Puritans by "lively
Applications . . . unto the Service of God." Mather
deemed the work "as laborious as any" but experienced
"a most wonderful Presence of God . . . in this Undertaking." Likewise, Thomas Hooker, who set apart Mon-
days to talk with "all sorts of Persons" at Hartford,
Connecticut, "sharply reproved" the lethargic and
hypocritical "with Fear, pulling them out of the Fire"
that eventually they would "be found in the Faith."[9]

Although the span of topics that ministers

handled during these sessions was vast, ranging from simple doubts about God's existence to the finer points of eschatology, the subject of witchcraft most deserves careful scrutiny. Not only does it illustrate how involved ministers became with their people when disseminating theology in practical contexts, but their handling of witchcraft reveals the extent to which there was a gap between Puritanism and what social historians call "peasant mentality" or "non-institutional, popular religion." Of course, there was some gap between pastors and laity or ministers would have been working in their libraries rather than visiting parishioners to establish collective mentality in New England. Take the case of the wife of one Thomas Witterridge. Since she was in "great horror," because a fortune-teller had predicted she should "meet with great trouble," Richard Hubbard, who ministered near Wenham, read her "several scriptures" to discredit or perhaps counter such prophesies but to no avail. That night she went berserk and ran off shrieking "thrō the thickest places of weeds and briars" and ended up drowned in "a little puddle of water not sufficient to cover her face." Similarly, John Hale of Beverly was unsuccessful in reforming Dorcas Hoar, a parishioner who confessed in 1670 that she had a book of palmistry. Though Hale told her that "it was an evil book and evil art," and she seemed to "renounce or reject all such practices," Hale subsequently discovered that Hoar still practiced the craft for malefic ends. Moreover, to conceal the fact that she had stolen "goods" from Hale's parsonage, Hoar intimidated Hale's twelve-year-old daughter, Rebecca, by threatening to "raise the Devil to kill her or bewitch her." But how chasmic was this rift in the collective culture of the region? How much difference was there between lay and ministerial thinking? Maybe it was only an emotional gap in Witterridge's case, and thus just her unstable reaction to Puritan dogma was atypical. Certainly Chadwick Hansen's data in Witchcraft at Salem (1969) about psychosomatic deaths supports such an interpretation. And in Hoar's case, despite her dabbling in palmistry, she did use Puritan demonology to influence Rebecca Hale, an indication Hoar understood ministerial doctrines.[10]

The crux of the matter, as historians since Robert Calef, a Boston merchant and hostile critic of Cotton Mather, have pointed out, lies in how much ministers promoted superstition. Miller, who thought

the intellectual history of New England could almost
be written without reference to witchcraft, embraced
the judgment of George Lyman Kittredge in Witchcraft
in Old and New England (1929) that the clergy's views
on witchcraft were "scientifically rational." Social
historians, too, have accepted this Revisionist position about the clergy but also argue that the laity
held folk beliefs about magic that rivaled Puritanism.
For instance, Jon Butler insists that to "understand
what many colonists meant by religion" historians
must "examine the survival of European occult or
magical practices in the American colonies, especially astrology, divination, and witchcraft." Common
sense suggests there is an element of truth in Butler's thesis, for traditions held in contempt by the
educated flourish among the masses of any era. And
Witterridge did respond differently to fortune-telling
than Hubbard, as did the girls at Salem Village when
compared to Samuel Parris, their local minister.
Much evidence, however, indicates that Puritan divines
were almost as credulous as their parishioners; even
an urbane Boston minister like Thomas Prince was "apt
to give too much credit, especially to surprising
stories." Furthermore, some facts point to the clergy
as promoters of European occultism, the very folk beliefs that drove Witterridge to hysteria.[11]

For example, John Higginson, the minister at
Salem Town, was not scientifically rational when he
reported that the Devil disguised himself as a human
and delivered a "Conjuring Book" to two men which,
when they read it, caused "Horror" and their hair to
stand on end. Or when he declared that a rich man
traded his soul to the Devil for a reputation of
"wisdome all the country over." These stories, and
Higginson deemed them "to be certain," indicate no
gap between him and Mrs. Witterridge about magic, except in response. And the fact that Increase Mather
collected such tales and published them in Remarkable
Providences (1684) shows that in the matter of witchcraft the clergy promoted belief in magical super-
naturalism not the scientific method of Newton.
Cotton Mather, as did many ministers, even interpreted
common natural occurrences magically; when "Many Hail-
Stones broke throw the Glass and flew to the middle
of the Room" in Samuel Sewall's house, where Mather
happened to be dining, his prayer that "we might be
ready for the time when our Clay-Tabernacles should be
broken" must have only reinforced Sewall's fears about
this "awfull Providence."[12]

Thus, Butler's distinction between magic and Christianity as different "subsets of the same phenomenon--religion," and his argument that the laity held to the former and the clergy to the latter, failed to recognize that these religions had always been intertwined. Even Kittredge admitted this when he wrote: "So intertwisted were Christianity and paganism that even the Pater Noster itself was treated by learned and pious men in a manner that approaches witchcraft." More recently, Keith Thomas found that in the sixteenth century belief in "a personal Satan" took on "a reality and immediacy which could not fail to grip the strongest mind. Influential preachers filled the ears of their hearers with tales of diabolic intervention in daily life." Ministers and stable laymen lived with these fuzzy notions overlapping Providence and the Devil's power without psychologically unraveling. That insecure personalities and immature people, as Hansen has shown, became hysterical in certain situations, and others like Dorcas Hoar, who used whatever served their purpose, further documents the amalgamation of vying traditions and in no way jeopardizes the existence of collective culture in New England.13

Likewise, the care that pastors gave the victims of witchcraft reveals little difference between the thinking of Puritan divines and their parishioners. In treating Elizabeth Knapp, a Lancaster girl who in 1671 suffered fits from seeing "Devills, in their hellish shapes," Samuel Willard reflected and reinforced both ministerial and folk traditions about Faustian pacts. In fact, Willard repeatedly pressured Knapp until she confessed before several onlookers to having wished the "Devill would come to her" that she might "give herselfe up to him soul and body." At one point, and Willard periodically visited Knapp for at least six months, he actually conversed with the Devil with Knapp as the medium. "Oh! you are a great roague . . . you tell the people a company of lyes," the grim voice told Willard. "Satan, thou are a lyar & a deceiver, & God will vindicate his own truth one day," Willard shot back. "I am not Satan, I am a pretty blacke boy, this is my pretty girle . . . . Oh! you black Roague, I do not love you." To which Willard ejaculated: "I hate thee." Eventually, the spectators joined in and told the voice, "God had him in chaines." The voice responded: "For all my chaine I can knocke thee on the head when I please." Another layman retorted: "But God is stronger than

22

thou." "That's a ly, I am stronger then God," groaned the voice. Horrified by such blasphemy, Willard halted the dialogue and advised everyone to be "wary of speaking" and to get "serious persons to watch with her & left her, comending her to God." That Willard made numerous trips to visit Knapp and engaged in what even he in a moment of insight called "preposterous courses" clearly debunks the notion of ministers as cloistered savants, revealing instead clergymen who participated in noninstitutional religious practices as they strove to make New England more puritanical.[14]

The actions of Cotton Mather also indicate little gap between folk superstitions and clerical thought. When in 1688 he took one of the children of John Goodwin, a Boston mason, into the parsonage to rescue her from "hellish Witchcraft," Mather's methods were magical rather than scientific. For example, when the girl was unable to read the Bible, he decided to learn more about pneumatology, the study of spiritual beings, by bringing her about a dozen books to see if she could read them. Mather happily discovered that she could read a Quaker book, The Oxford Jests, and a work denying the existence of witches, whereas volumes like Willard's Treatise of Justification or Cotton's Milk for Babes would "bring hideous Convulsions on the Child if she look't into them." Similarly, Mather ran other tests, too complicated to describe briefly, on the girl to see if demons could read his mind, which led him to believe that "all Devils are not alike sagacious." Regarding these and other experiments, Mather declared: "I confess I have Learn't much more than I sought, and I have bin informed of some things relating to the invisible World, which as I did not think it lawful to ask, so I do not think it proper to tell." Such discoveries led Mather four years later to have a dialogue, including pantomime, with Mercy Short, a Boston servant girl, that smacked of credulity. When she claimed demons stopped her from hearing him speak the words "Jesus Christ" and the "Old Serpents Head," Mather supposedly fooled the devils by substituting "an Old Snake" for serpent, pointing heavenward for Christ, and striking his forehead with his finger to symbolize Christ's victory over Satan. "Oh! I understand," Short responded to such antics.[15]

The point is not to discredit the clergy as benighted dupes, as Progressive historians did, but to show ministers shared a collective culture with laymen. Understandably, Harvard Revisionists ignored this ministerial participation in mass culture, as they countered Progressive diatribes by emphasizing the intellectual ties of the clergy with the best minds of their day. Social historians, readily accepting the Revisionist picture of an isolated clergy, widened the gap between classes by divorcing the folk traditions of laymen from the ministers' world of print. But the behavior of pastors demonstrates a bridging of folk and elite worlds.

Such bridging is especially apparent in the way ministers handled accused witches, both reflecting and leading lay New Englanders. Adhering to folklore, preachers believed in witches and attributed great powers to them, but because of their ties to the intellectual world of European rationalism, they opposed the obsolete thinking and cultural lag among ordinary people. Thus, Puritan divines warned parishioners against outdated tests to determine a witch's guilt, such as trial by water where the witch was tied, cast into a pond, and declared innocent if she sank. Likewise, they rejected the test of reciting the Lord's prayer without error or being able to weep at heart-rending spectacles, as well as proofs like the witch's tit, the touch test, and spectral evidence. They repudiated white magic, too, such as the witch cake or the boiling of urine, but not because they doubted its power; rather it was, as Cotton Mather warned, invoking a "Devil's shield against a Devil's sword." Confession buttressed by corroborating details, the testimony of trustworthy witnesses about supernatural feats, and the discovery of the tools of the witch's trade, that is, images, potions, and magic books, were the respectable proofs of witchcraft among seventeenth-century thinkers everywhere, and these the ministers endorsed. New England divines, therefore, were not in an ivory tower but participants with laymen in a cultural web that mixed European folk traditions, Puritan theology, and new philosophical trends.[16]

This merging of classes, both reflecting and promoting collective mentality, is even more evident in the daily assistance that ministers gave to laymen encountering life's mundane troubles, as Cotton Mather eulogized about one faithful shepherd: "If any of his Neighborhood were in distress, he was like a Brother born for their Adversity." Familial problems often drew ministers deeply into the domestic affairs of their parishioners. When parents were at "grievous Variance" with children, pastors appeared to heal breaches and "bring the Family into a better Condition." Cotton Mather consoled one Rebecca Brown because her "foolish Son" put her in "extreme Danger of being hurried into the Grave." Mather advised parishioners in such cases to guard against the "Grief and Wrath" that arises from a damaged reputation, adore and accept "divine Sovereignty," repent for their sins and those of the child, and use effectual methods for the "Dispossession of an Evil Spirit." Similarly, Peter Thacher labored at least a month in 1685 with Sergeant Vose of Milton and his daughter, Jane, who were quarreling over her engagement to Peter Lion. Shuttling between the estranged parties, Thacher encouraged Vose to "consent that P. Lion should marry his daughter," and that failing, Thacher tried to "take off her affections." Then he "labored much" with Peter and Jane together. Though Thacher neglected to record the outcome, such counseling shows his influence upon and participation in the daily life of the laity. So does another case involving a "great Affliction, by a Daughter violently sett upon a Match," because Cotton Mather reported: "They all cast themselves into my Hands to help them; and I will gladly give what Help I can unto them." Even when children were away from home, there could be problems that made ministers a force in the world of laymen. Cotton Mather once comforted a "poor pious, praying widow" whose two sons had deserted from Annapolis, laboring to "make her Heart sing for Joy" and deliver the boys from their "unhappy circumstances."[17]

Husbands and wives battled too, and ministers intervened to "sweeten their Spirits towards each other." One time such sweetening involved a "well-contrived" letter from Cotton Mather to a certain "abominable Fellow" who intolerably abused his "godly, humble, patient Wife." To help another wife, whose husband was "entangled with another Woman . . . in another Countrey," again Mather wrote to the man and exhorted him to return home and do penance. Nehemiah Walter of Roxbury worked long and hard to reunite Samuel Sewall, Jr., and his adulterous wife, Rebeckah. Even after a three-year separation and the birth of a bastard son to Rebeckah, Walter continued to advise Samuel "to his going home to his wife." In this particular case, the parents helped Walter to effect eventually a reconciliation; but when bumptious in-laws meddled in bad marriages, pastors had a more difficult time restoring harmony. "A gracious Woman in my Neighbourhood," Cotton Mather lamented, "almost kill'd with a froward Husband, and other abominable Relatives; her Case calls for much Commiseration with me."[18]

Eventually heads of household grew old and "Ripe for Heaven," often suffering from illness, poverty, and loneliness. Thus ministers were "much in their Company," deeming it "pure Religion, to visit the Widow and the Orphan." Cotton Mather, who tried "every Week" to visit "headless Families," wrote a consoling poem for one "aged and pious Gentlewoman, visited with total Blindness," and to assist an elderly man with a "grievous Distraction," Mather rallied "pious Neighbors to meet and pray" for him and furnished "other Compassions to him and his Family." During the winter, Mather preached to aged shut-ins at the Boston almshouse who were unable to brave the cold and attend church services. Joseph Green even traveled from Salem Village to Reading to visit one Deacon Fitch who was "almost blind, and old Mr. Weston quite blind, and other disconsolate deaf, &c." Samuel Willard and Judge Sewall went from Boston to Plymouth to visit "loansom" Samuel Torrey, who took their visit "very kindly" and at dinner "made Mr. Willard crave a blessing and return Thanks."[19]

When death took a member of the family, whether old or young, the pastor was again drawn closely to his parishioners as the "frequent and welcome Comforter of the Mourners." Routinely spreading Puritan ideas among the laity, preachers exhorted their charges to "say and pray, Father in Heaven, thy Will be done" but also permitted mourners to grieve without feeling guilty. "Lamentations are not Amiss," taught Cotton Mather, "We must not be Sticks and Stones." Likewise, Colman warned against the "Danger of Grief when too much suppressed," urging mourners to "freely give vent to your Thoughts." Ministers only frowned on "Immoderate Mourners" who grieved too much, as Cotton Mather put it: "Do not Sorrow as others, that have no Hope." That laymen welcomed such ministerial advice and attention was apparent when Solomon Stoddard of Northampton sent a letter of condolence to Samuel Sewall after his first wife, Hannah, died. The Judge "soked it in Tears at reading" and deemed the "Letter to be an Answer to my Prayer for God's gracious looking upon me." The attendant pastor could be moved at such times, too,

as when Henry Gibbs of Watertown recalled in a funeral
sermon on the wife of William Robie of Boston: "The
many Days I spent in your Family, when my Bodily in-
dispositions prevented from Publick Service, afforded
me such Occasions of Converse with her, that her Memory will be always Precious to me." From cradle to
grave, then, family life pulled the clergy and laity
into a collective culture shaped by ministerial counsel.[20]

Social historians have rightly identified a con-
tentiousness among New Englanders that sometimes made
relations between neighbors "downright abrasive" but,
like the Revisionists, have largely ignored the
clergy's practical efforts among laymen to maintain
peaceable kingdoms. For example, John Hancock, who
could "root out the Seeds of Discord when sown among
Brethren and Neighbors," quickly resolved boundary
disputes between laymen by calling the contenders together, going to the debated ground, listening to
their arguments, examining the premises, and then
ordering them to cut stakes. "Now drive that stake
there," Hancock would command, "and pile some stones
around it, and another there." With all the stakes
in place, Hancock announced: "There is your line;
let there be no more quarreling; go home and live in
peace, and serve God." Hancock never could have commanded such respect--even allowing for hagiographical
exaggeration--simply as a Harvard graduate who preached
erudite sermons on Sunday, and his style was not that
of a genteel elitist living outside folk culture. His
kind of power accrued to a man who on a regular basis,
and for a long period of time, wisely counseled his
people on a variety of matters, a preacher who shared
a common culture with parishioners. In contrast,
Ebenezer Parkman, fresh from Harvard, failed to recon-
cile Asher Rice and Josiah Newton, two Westborough
residents. "Instead of healing," Parkman lamented
after one session with them, "new work was made" when
Rice accused Newton of having "a principle of falsehood
in his heart." Even though Rice eventually was "Sorry
for what he had said," Parkman saw "little prospect of
Concord or Composition." And at Salem where factions
riddled the community, a succession of ministers, as
Boyer and Nissenbaum have shown, could not stop the
"quarreling and smiting." Such difficulties led Joseph
Baxter of Medfield to conclude that ministers never had
"more need to manage themselves more wisely and prudently than when they see strife," because if such con-
flicts "be not then wisely and prudently managed things

27

will grow worse and worse." But even in failure pastors were obviously out among the people, shaping a common culture and trying like Robert Breck of Marlborough to bring the contentious into "a pacifick Sea, by the Conduct of Heaven."[21]

While healing the feuds in families and between neighbors brought pastors into contact with many New Englanders, the clergy's care for those in need of medical attention was even more widespread. According to Daniel J. Boorstin, there was hardly "a religious leader of the region who did not dispense medical knowledge." Medicine in the seventeenth century, as Malcolm Sydney Beinfield explained, was not "a profession in itself, but rather an avocation . . . relegated to the preacher . . . who could devote sufficient time to intellectual pursuits." Indeed, over 9% of all Puritan divines in New England were full-fledged physicians, and most rural pastors were like James Noyes of Stonington, curing the sick "partly by his Recipe's & partly by his Prayers," yet another example of the blending of folkways with Puritanism. Even ministers like Cotton Mather, who lived in towns with full-time doctors, dispensed "noble Remedies" on visits to the ailing and, because of their combining of practical and intellectual pursuits, published medical treatises. In fact, Thomas Thacher of Boston wrote the first medical treatise published in America, A Brief Rule to Guide the Common-People of New-England How to Order Themselves and Theirs in the Small Pocks, or Measles (1678).

This "Angelic Conjunction," as Cotton Mather called the linking of medicine and divinity, enabled clergymen to permeate lay culture with Puritanism. James Noyes "went every where to the Poor as well as to the Rich," and at their bedside he was "more like a Father than a Physician," encouraging, counseling, and fervently praying with his patients. One especially colorful account of Hugh Adams's delivery of a baby documents how clerical physicians combined religion and medicine. About midnight he went to help Mary Glitten, one of his parishioners at Durham, New Hampshire. He first prayed, quoting I Timothy 2:15 that "the woman shall be saved in child bearing &c." Then he administered "strong Hysterick medicines" to quicken labor, dilated her "passage of nature with Unguentum Aperitivum meipsum," and proceeded manually to deliver the infant. Discovering the baby's "most unusual and improbable posture" for birth, Adams cried to Christ for "Immediate Direction and Help in that Extremity," whereupon he moved the child into "capable posture." Concluding that the newborn's life "appeared doubtfull," Adams then baptized the baby. Though Cotton Mather did not deliver babies, he did visit pregnant women, exhorting them to prepare for their "dying hour," meditate on the "precious promises of God," and make "their Circumstances an awakening Occasion to settle the Peace of their Souls."[22]

Calling on the sick, which regularly brought all ministers face to face with New Englanders "whether of his own congregation, or not," also spread Puritanism everywhere. For example, when a family whom Cotton Mather deemed "Quaker and High Church and a little Atheistical" fell ill, he jumped to "visit them, and releeve them and instruct them, and do all the Good that is possible for them." Mather usually entered sickrooms armed with a Puritan litany that urged sufferers to repent of the immorality which caused the illness, resign cheerfully to Providence, and plead for deliverance from sin not illness. Others were more empathetic, as when Samuel Dexter of Dedham spontaneously sang Psalms with a dying man or when Thomas Shepard told John Collins: "Young Man, thou shalt not dye but live; but remember, that now the Lord says, Surely, thou wilt now fear Him, and receive instruction." Such opportunities multiplied greatly during epidemics, drawing ministers even closer to all their townspeople. John Bishop of Stamford, Connecticut, reported in 1676: "We have been all down & some of us dangerously sick, but graciously restored. We buried 6 [?] in one week in our little town; neer 20 this spring; about an 100 sick at once." During numerous outbreaks at Boston, Cotton Mather recorded that his time was "pretty much spent among the sick and weak," praying with as many as twenty-two families a day and leaving him "exceedingly tired" and with "little Time to study." To ensure the gospel would not be forgotten by laymen after their recovery, preachers like Samuel Danforth of Roxbury reminded the healed: "Well, you have been in God's School, but what have you learnt?" Whatever the response, ministers undoubtedly reinforced earlier lessons, as when Bishop declared: "The Lord is righteous in all His awfull dispensacons throughout the Country, as we must acknowledg, with submission, and studdy reformacon of life & maners . . . for the p[r]venting of further evils & calamities."[23]

29

Of course, parishioners did not always recuperate, and consequently pastors helped them prepare to die and instructed their friends and relatives, who were likely to be receptive to Puritanism at such a stressful time. Given the recent arguments of David E. Stannard, which he derived from sermons, about the Puritans' fear of death, it would seem that pastors must have often quelled the anxieties of the dying. But actual cases of deathbed encounters between laity and clergy do not bear out Stannard's thesis. To be sure, ministers did encounter some parishioners fearful about the "King of Terrors." Governor John Winthrop wrote about the dying of the wife of one Onion of Roxbury: "She fell withal into great horror and trembling, so as it shook the room, etc., and crying out . . . that she neglected her spiritual good for a little worldly trash, and now she must go to everlasting torments." Even though someone, probably John Eliot of Roxbury, urged her to consider "God's infinite mercy," she replied: "I cannot for my life." Yet, many New Englanders faced death calmly and without any apparent fears. According to William Homes of Chilmark, one Abigail Smith suffered acutely on her deathbed but still evinced a "good hope . . . of her future well being." Individuals as different as Cotton Mather's first wife, Abigail; John Saffin, a prominent Bostonian; and Nathaniel Rogers, the minister of Ipswich, also experienced inner peace in the face of death. Perhaps their last words exuded as much confidence as those of John Bailey of Watertown: "Oh! my Lord Jesus Christ is altogether lovely! All our praises of Him here, are poor and low Things! His glorious Angels are come for mee!" Such "excellent Souls," according to Cotton Mather, had triumphed over the "Sting and Fear of Death."[24]

Other deathbed scenes provide no support for Stannard's thesis and reveal instead that pastors utilized different ministrations to meet individual needs and promote collective culture. Cotton Mather used "sacred Hilaritie" to cheer one fellow, asking him: "Have you thought, what to say, when you arrive among the blessed Angels? Hee replied: Why, pray, what do you intend to say? I answer'd . . . I'l say, Oh! yee Illustrious Angels, if you don't wonderfully glorifie the Grace of the Lord Jesus Christ, in fetching so vile a Sinner into these Mansions, you'l never do it!" Samuel Willard had only to pray and hold the hand of Daniel Quincy, Samuel Sewall's cousin, to comfort the man before he "quietly expired." In contrast, Samuel Fiske of Salem had to listen to Hannah Dean repent of the "Sin of Fornication" and shortly after her death negotiate her "desire to be reconciled to the Church." James Allen of Boston, who had prepared the will of Bellingham, Governor of Massachusetts, "some years before his Death," had to help finalize that will at Bellingham's deathbed, as well as agree to become "one of the Executors." And Increase Mather, roused from a warm bed late one September night in 1675, probably heeded the dying pleas of Leonard Hoar, President of Harvard, who asked Mather to educate young John Hoar, Leonard's nephew, and effect a reconciliation between John and his father.[25]

Because of confident declarations by parishioners like Bailey and the absence of fear about dying among many others, Stannard's argument that nearly everyone reacted similarly to dying in "Puritan New England" seems faulty. Stannard countered such criticism-- first advanced by Frederick F. Harling of Westfield State College--by arguing that the "rhapsodizing" expressions of dying Puritans are a leftover rhetoric from medieval Christianity. In short, we are not to take their statements of confidence literally but rather read between the lines. Yet, Stannard built his case on a literal interpretation of the speeches which support his thesis; and given the Puritan view that to doubt one's salvation is a sign of grace, as Stannard himself described in his article and subsequent book, there is also good reason not to take the Puritans' "Horror of being Deceived at the last" too literally. Even Stannard admitted that there might be genuine exceptions to his thesis, arguing that he was aware of them but still "struck by certain remarkably consistent patterns in Puritan thought and action when facing the problem of death." Yet, he never incorporated such exceptions into his analysis but merely substituted his monolithic generalization about Puritans fearing death for an earlier view advanced by Perry Miller and Allan I. Ludwig that monolithically attributed "cosmic optimism" to dying New Englanders. The pastoral work of ministers, however, shows that the best methodology is to interpret all the evidence literally, allowing some latitude for rhetorical devices and theological notions, and conclude that Puritans reacted differently to a common ideology.[26]

If any New Englanders were peasants and likely

to be isolated from elites, surely they lived among
the poor. But the poor, like the sick and dying,
were often in close contact with ministers who strove
to be "shining examples of liberality to the poor,
and pour down their <u>alms</u> like the showers of Heaven
upon them." Indeed, preachers did give across-the-
board assistance to the needy, whether a "very pious"
woman in South Boston or a "forlorn, froward, wicked
old Man, perishing in an helpless old Age, and the
want of every thing." Such charity touched the lives
of orphans, widows, unwed mothers, criminals, blacks,
native Americans, the aged, the sick, and the men-
tally ill. Usually the clergy helped the poor individually, as when Andrew Gardner, Jr., of Worcester
went so far as to give away his "only pair of shoes"
to a needy parishioner, leaving the parson to "of-
ficiate in stocking feet or borrowed slippers." However, when widespread calamities, such as fires, epidemics, famines, bitter winters, and wars, ravaged
New Englanders, preachers assisted the victims <u>en</u>
<u>masse</u>. For example, Hugh Peter of Salem, an affluent
"man of a very public spirit," helped the whole Bay
Colony in 1636 when he purchased a shipload of goods
"at fifty in the hundred, (which saved the country
£200,) and distributed them to all the towns, as each
town needed." After one Boston fire, Cotton Mather
dispensed "so many Kindnesses" that he saw no reason
to record "particular Instances" in his diary. And
in 1696 when a "Harvest so failed" in Massachusetts
that a "<u>terrible Famine</u>" plagued the Bay Colony poor,
Mather <u>drew up a moving</u> petition, endorsed by other
pastors, which appealed to Connecticut clergymen to
request their government to "remitt the <u>Embargo</u>" on
corn. Mather also made it his "Duty, to bee much in
<u>Fasting</u> before the Lord" to "procure <u>Food</u>" for his
distressed neighbors.[27]

Seeking always to disseminate Puritan doctrines
among the masses, ministers used their largess to instruct believers and convert sinners; as Cotton
Mather put it: "Who can tell, but in this Way of
treating such poor Creatures, there may be some won
over to the Ways of Piety!" Thus, ministers like
Mather, and he was typical, would help a "poor Man
clothed with Rags" and then "rebuke him, and exhort
him." If such recipients were already converted,
Mather urged them to build their faith by offering
this prayer: "<u>O my Heavenly Father, and continual</u>
<u>Feeder</u> . . . <u>Thou knowest, I have need of those things</u>
<u>which I am to Eat, and to Drink, and to be cloathed</u>

withal . . . . I now trust in thee, that thou wilt not Suffer me or mine, to want anything that shall be Good for us." Other ministers similarly exhorted sinners to repent, forsake their vices, and in John Cotton's words to "be carefull to come better out of affliction then you went in." For example, after criminals suffered the "just Sentence of Authority," John Wilson of Boston combined "his Bounty" with "gracious Admonitions" to make them "remarkably penitent." Even in his will Theophilus Cotton of Hampton Falls, New Hampshire, made one bequest contingent on progress in piety, leaving a piece of plate worth £5 to the people of Shoals if they gathered a church within three years.[28]

This strategy of maintaining a Puritan collective culture by providing "Tenderness both to the Souls & Bodies of men" is perhaps best illustrated by ministerial aid to education, for according to Benjamin Colman there was "no Sort of Charity more acceptable to God, and beneficial to our Country, than an early and pious Education of Youth." Samuel Lee, who ministered at Bristol among "spirituall beares in Rhode Island," actually tied a request for a teacher to his cultural goals, explaining to Increase Mather that if someone would support a tutor for the children of a Malta gentleman, there was hope for proselytism of the family. Similarly, Joseph Green is representative of those who sponsored the erection of a schoolhouse and hiring of an instructor to reach all the youth of a town. Green first spoke privately with certain townspeople, securing land from one Deacon Ingersoll and additional support from others "willing to help it forward," and then publicly appealed to Salem villagers at a town meeting to embrace this "opportunity for so good a service." Subsequently, he gathered timber and helped build the structure. Months after its completion, Green continued "hurying about ye school house," paying dame Deland her salary and making sure the students learned "everything that is good." At Boston, where schools always existed for those with money, ministers eventually sponsored "CHARITY SCHOOLS," for the "Instruction and godly Education of poor Boys, the other of poor Girls." Cotton Mather promised the "Gift of a Bible, to such of the children at the Charity-Schole as become able readily to read a chapter in it." And Mather rewarded students at the Boston grammar school with money for mastering "by heart, the Maxims of the Everlasting Gospel," in Mather's Lapis e Monte Excisus (1716).

33

He even set up schools for blacks and Indians of all ages that they might "learn to read, and be instructed in the Catechism." Charity, therefore, provided the "vehicles" through which ministers could engage the poor in "certain exercises of piety," guarantee their exposure to Puritanism, and foster collective culture.[29]

Obviously, by catechizing, leading parishioners to grace and church membership, combating witchcraft, helping families, keeping peace between neighbors, tending the sick and dying, aiding the poor, and promoting education, over the years Puritan divines repeatedly bombarded most, if not all, New Englanders with the gospel. But how many laymen truly embraced Puritanism to form the collective culture sponsored by ministers? It is, of course, impossible to determine exactly; as Morison once quipped "too bad that no one had the bright idea to circulate the following questionnaire...Why did you come to New England?... Are you a church member?...Check preferred denomination...." While a few historians--Pope, Ross W. Beales, Jr., and Gerald F. Moran--have more recently managed to estimate the number of new communicants admitted to certain seventeenth-century congregations, especially after mid-century, comprehensive statistics about the number of Puritans in New England are still unavailable. And it is doubtful, given the paucity of records, that Puritan scholars could ever duplicate the estimates that Patricia V. Bonomi and Peter R. Eisenstadt compiled for eighteenth-century America. Moreover, even if we could determine what percentage of the population attended church, the key question of genuine commitment to Puritanism, which has occupied observers since the first jeremiad, would remain unanswered. Thus, we are left with the traditional anecdotal method; and though it cannot quantify the number of New England Puritans, it can reveal how effective pastoral encounters were as a means to spreading a collective Puritan culture.[30]

Certainly face-to-face counseling did not work with everyone. As already shown, laymen like Dorcas Hoar wilfully flouted John Hale's exhortations, and others, such as Onion's wife or Mrs. Witterridge, for unknown reasons profited nothing from ministerial instruction. They were not alone. As early as 1638, Dorothy Talbye of Salem, condemned for infanticide, refused the counsel of Hugh Peter and John Wilson, both of whom accompanied her to the execution site but "could do no good with her." Likewise, in 1690, freeman John Hurd, a crusty tailor who had liked his liquor, spurned the deathbed advice of two pastors, allowing them to pray for him only after considerable badgering by his wife and the ministers themselves. Even when Sarah Good of Salem Village, who was utterly destitute and begging for food and shelter, received aid from Samuel Parris, her only response was to walk off "muttering."[31]

Despite such cases, there is much more evidence to indicate that laymen responded positively to the personal influence of a pastoral call. Many a criminal, like James Morgan, a condemned murderer, asked a visiting minister: "Is there not Mercy for me in Christ?" And then the preacher led the receptive prisoner through an abbreviated morphology of conversion. The people of Scituate "delighted to see" Nathaniel Eells "at their door, as he rode up on horseback to inquire after their health, and took pleasure in taking his pipe to light." Likewise, John Wise of Essex was well received; "no man ever went out of his Presence Sorrowful," and even his critics admired his "Majesty mixt with Affability." There are also stories about how someone "drawing near his End" miraculously recovered during a pastoral call, as when Cotton Mather attended one Mr. Avery. "In the very Time of my Prayer," wrote Mather, "the good Man, felt as it were a Load, or Cloud, beginning to roll off his Spirits; and came abroad shortly, unto the Glory of God." Such examples could be multiplied manyfold, and this entire chapter has documented the many close and warm ties between laity and ministry. Indeed, from my reading of the sources, the admiring people of Scituate and those like Mr. Avery were more typical of New Englanders than either Dorcas Hoar or John Hurd.[32]

The issue, however, is further complicated by the changes over time in New England society. As shown in the final chapter, certain New Englanders steadily became more secular and others turned to dissenting religions--a Puritan to Yankee trend that continuously offered ever more alternatives to Puritanism. Yet whatever percentage of people were Puritans in 1630, 1660, or 1690, and it will never be known precisely, the gulf between ministers and laymen did not gape because pastors were intellectual elites and isolated from commoners. On the contrary, the pastoral work of ministers among all segments of the population enabled them to influence significantly the religious, social, and political culture of New England. To be sure, for a variety of reasons with the passage of time, more and more people rejected the clergy and opted for either folk traditions, new religions, or avant-garde philosophies in lieu of Puritanism. Or, more typically, they mixed them all together, constantly eroding the tenuous homogeneity of the original settlers of New England. Nonetheless, because pastors did so often come into contact with almost all New Englanders, it is likely that many laymen accepted in varying degrees ministerial ideas. And to that unquantifiable extent New Englanders shared a collective Puritan culture, sustaining it until about the end of the seventeenth century when a majority of the population shifted the balance to dissenting religions, secular pursuits, and Enlightenment philosophies.

Notes

1. Miller, The New England Mind: The Seventeenth
   Century, 21; Youngs, "Perry Miller and the
   'Buzzing Factuality' of Colonial New England,"
   18; Morgan to Selement, December 13, 1982;
   Rutman, "The Mirror of Puritan Authority," in
   McGiffert, ed., Puritanism, 78; Butler, "Magic,"
   317, 320; McGiffert, "American Puritan Studies
   in the 1960's," 59. For the most recent state-
   ment of differences between social and intellectual historians about collective culture, see the
   responses of Darrett B. Rutman and David D. Hall
   to my "The Meeting of Elite and Popular Minds at
   Cambridge, New England, 1638-1645," William and
   Mary Quarterly, forthcoming in 1984.

2. McGiffert, "American Puritan Studies in the
   1960's," 38; Cotton Mather, Magnalia Christi
   Americana; or, the Ecclesiastical History of New
   England (London, 1702),Book III, 26, 144, 56;
   Increase Mather, The Life and Death of that Rev-
   erend Man of God, Mr. Richard Mather (Cambridge,
   Mass., 1670), 33; M. G. Hall, ed., "The Autobiog-
   raphy of Increase Mather," American Antiquarian
   Society, Proceedings, LXXI (1961), 350; Samuel
   Mather, The Life of the Very Reverend and Learned
   Cotton Mather (Boston, 1729), 110; Israel Loring,
   Ministers Must Certainly and Shortly Die (Boston,
   1731), 14.

3. Colman, The Prophet's Death Lamented (Boston,
   1723), 33; Mather, Magnalia, Book IV, 190, 174;
   Edmund S. Morgan, ed., The Diary of Michael
   Wigglesworth, 1653-1657; The Conscience of a
   Puritan (New York, 1965), v-vii, 71; Cotton
   Mather, A Faithful Man, Described and Rewarded
   (Boston, 1705), 26.

4. Samuel A. Green, ed., "Diary of Increase Mather,"
   Massachusetts Historical Society, Proceedings,
   2nd Ser., XIII (1899-1900), 347, 365, hereafter
   cited M.H.S.; John Langdon Sibley and Clifford K.
   Shipton, Sibley's Harvard Graduates: Biographical
   Sketches of Those Who Attended Harvard College
   (Cambridge, Mass., 1873-1975), I, 433, III, 435-
   436; hereafter cited as Sibley's Harvard Graduates; Appleton, The Servant's Actual Readiness for
   the Coming of the Lord (Boston, 1752), 32; Miller,
   The New England Mind, vii.

5. Mather, <u>Magnalia</u>, Book III, 103; Mather, <u>Boni-</u>
    <u>facius: An Essay upon the Good</u> (1710), edited
    by David Levin (Cambridge, Mass., 1966), 74;
    Cotton Mather, <u>Ratio Disciplinae Fratrum Nov-</u>
    <u>Anglorum</u> (Boston, 1726), 105; <u>Sibley's Harvard</u>
    <u>Graduates</u>, III, 163; Robert G. Pope, ed., <u>The</u>
    <u>Notebook of the Reverend John Fiske, 1644-1675</u>
    (Boston, 1974), 186-187.

6. Benjamin Wadsworth, <u>A Guide for the Doubting</u>
    (Boston, 1711), preface; M. Halsey Thomas, ed.,
    <u>The Diary of Samuel Sewall, 1674-1729</u> (New York,
    1973), I, 345-346.

7. Mather, <u>Magnalia</u>, Book III, 84; Morgan, <u>Diary of</u>
    <u>Michael Wigglesworth</u>, 110-113.

8. Thomas, ed., <u>Diary of Samuel Sewall</u>, I, 418, 16,
    26, 33-40; "Thacher's Journal" in A. K. Teele,
    <u>The History of Milton, Mass., 1640-1887</u> (Boston,
    1887), Appendix B, 654; Worthington Chauncey
    Ford, ed., <u>Diary of Cotton Mather</u> (New York,
    1957), II, 506, I, 104.

9. Mather, <u>The Cure of Sorrow</u> (Boston, 1709), 38;
    Thomas, ed., <u>Diary of Samuel Sewall</u>, I, 39-40,
    603; Ford, ed., <u>Diary of Cotton Mather</u>, I, 114-
    115; Mather, <u>Magnalia</u>, Book III, 65.

10. Butler, "Magic," 317; "Memoir of the Rev. William
    Adams," M.H.S., <u>Collections</u>, 4th Ser., I (1852),
    17-18; Chadwick Hansen, <u>Witchcraft at Salem</u> (New
    York, 1969), 72-73.

11. Miller, <u>The New England Mind: From Colony to</u>
    <u>Province</u>, 191; Butler, "Magic," 318; Charles
    Chauncy, "A Sketch of Eminent Men in New England,"
    M.H.S., <u>Collections</u>, X (1890), 164.

12. John Higginson to Increase Mather, August 17,
    1683, M.H.S., <u>Collections</u>, 4th Ser., VIII, 285-
    286; Thomas, ed., <u>Diary of Samuel Sewall</u>, I,
    330-331.

13. Butler, "Magic," 319; George Lyman Kittredge,
    <u>Witchcraft in Old and New England</u> (Cambridge,
    Mass., 1929), 31; Thomas, <u>Religion and the De-</u>
    <u>cline of Magic</u> (New York, 1971), 470-471.

14. "Samuel Willard's Account of the Strange Case of

Elizabeth Knapp of Groton," M.H.S., Collections, 4th Ser., VIII, 558, 565-567.

15. George Lincoln Burr, ed., Narratives of the Witchcraft Cases, 1648-1706 (New York, 1914), 101, 112-113, 122-123, 272-273.

16. Increase Mather, An Essay for the Recording of Illustrious Providences (Boston, 1684), 245-288; Boyer and Nissenbaum, Salem Possessed, 9-21; Hansen, Witchcraft at Salem, 45-50, 79-81, 157-158.

17. Mather, Magnalia, Book III, 181; Ford, ed., Diary of Cotton Mather, II, 63, 765, 465-466, 69, 146; "Thacher's Journal," Teele, The History of Milton, 656.

18. Ford, ed., Diary of Cotton Mather, II, 133, 774, 80, 365; Thomas, ed., Diary of Samuel Sewall, II, 705 note 4, 886-887.

19. Mather, Magnalia, Book IV, 204; Ford, ed., Diary of Cotton Mather, I, 168, 408, II, 576, I, 178; Samuel P. Fowler and George Francis Dow, eds., "Diary of Rev. Joseph Green, of Salem Village," Essex Institute, Historical Collections, X (1869), 80; Thomas, ed., Diary of Samuel Sewall, I, 197-198.

20. Cotton Mather, The Comfortable Chambers (Boston, 1728), 25; Ebenezer Turell, The Life and Character of the Reverend Benjamin Colman, D.D. (Boston, 1749), 186-187; Cotton Mather, Wholesome Words (Boston, 1713), 23; Thomas, ed., Diary of Samuel Sewall, II, 872; Henry Gibbs, Bethany: Or, The House of Mourning (Boston, 1714), preface.

21. John Demos, "Underlying Themes in the Witchcraft of Seventeenth-Century New England," American Historical Review. LXXV (1970), 1319; Appleton, The Servant's Actual Readiness, 32; Sibley's Harvard Graduates, III, 434; Francis G. Walett, ed., The Diary of Ebenezer Parkman (Worcester, 1974), 29; Boyer and Nissenbaum, Salem Possessed, 45; J. William T. Youngs, Jr., God's Messengers: Religious Leadership in Colonial New England, 1700-1750 (Baltimore, 1976), 54; John Swift, A

Funeral Discourse Delivered at Marlborough (Boston, 1731), 14.

22. Boorstin, *The Americans: The Colonial Experience* (New York, 1958), 231; Beinfield, "The Early New England Doctor: An Adaptation to a Provincial Environment," *Yale Journal of Biology and Medicine*, XV (1942), 101; Eliphalet Adams, *Eminently Good and Useful Men* (New London, 1720), 39-40; Ford, ed., *Diary of Cotton Mather*, II, 590-591, 24; Hugh Adams, "A Narrative of Remarkable-Instances of A Particular-Faith, and Answers of Prayer," 35-36, M.H.S. Ms.; Levin, ed., *Bonifacius*, 74. I am indebted to Laurel Thatcher Ulrich for providing me with the anecdote about Hugh Adams.

23. John Cotton, *A Funeral Sermon Preach'd at Bristol* (Boston, 1729), 32; Ford, ed., *Diary of Cotton Mather*, II, 96, 105, 648, 652; Mather, *Wholesome Words*, 14-19; "Extracts from the Diary of Rev. Samuel Dexter, of Dedham," *New England Historical and Geneological Register*, XIII (1859), 306-307; Mather, *Magnalia*, Book III, 200, IV, 155; John Bishop to Increase Mather, May 8, 1676, M.H.S., *Collections*, 4th Ser., VIII, 299.

24. Stannard, "Death and Dying in Puritan New England," *American Historical Review*, LXXVIII (1973), 1317; James Kendall Hosmer, ed., *Winthrop's Journal: History of New England, 1630-1649* (New York, 1946), II, 93; "Diary of Rev. William Homes of Chilmark, Martha's Vineyard, 1689-1746," *New England Historical and Genealogical Register*, L (1896), 155-156; Ford, ed., *Diary of Cotton Mather*, I, 448-449, 244, II, 98; Thomas, ed., *Diary of Samuel Sewall*, II, 641; Mather, *Magnalia*, Book III, 108.

25. Ford, ed., *Diary of Cotton Mather*, I, 234; Thomas, ed., *Diary of Samuel Sewall*, I, 264; Richard D. Pierce, ed., *The Records of the First Church in Salem Massachusetts 1629-1736* (Salem, 1974), 261-262; Richard Bellingham, *A Copy of the Last Will and Testament of Richard Bellingham, Esqr.* ([Boston, 1706]), no pagination; Green, ed. "Diary of Increase Mather," 355.

26. Stannard, *The Puritan Way of Death: A Study in Religion, Culture, and Social Change* (New York,

1977), 78-79; Harling's criticism and Stannard's reply are in the American Historical Review, LXXIX (1974), 917-918. Gordon E. Geddes's Welcome Joy: Death in Puritan New England (Ann Arbor, 1981) presents much original material but avoids taking a stand on the historiographical differences between Miller, Ludwig, and Stannard.

27. Levin, ed., Bonifacius, 79; Ford, ed., Diary of Cotton Mather, II, 137, 556, 115, I, 223, 191-193; Sibley's Harvard Graduates, V, 639; Hosmer, ed., Winthrop's Journal, I, 178.

28. Ford, ed., Diary of Cotton Mather, I, 580, II, 335; Mather, The Cure of Sorrow, 39-40; Stephen Foster, Their Solitary Way: The Puritan Social Ethic in the First Century of Settlement in New England (New Haven, 1971), 129-130; Mather, Magnalia, Book III, 50; Sibley's Harvard Graduates, V, 37.

29. Adams, Eminently Good and Useful Men, 39; Turell, The Life and Character of the Reverend Benjamin Colman, D.D., 70-71; Samuel Lee to Increase Mather, August 14, 1687, M.H.S., Collections, 4th Ser., VIII, 541; Fowler and Dow, eds., "Diary of Rev. Joseph Green," 78-81, 84; Ford, ed., Diary of Cotton Mather, II, 373, 337, 379, 500; Levin, ed., Bonifacius, 78-79.

30. Morison, Builders of the Bay Colony, 341; Robert G. Pope, The Half-Way Covenant: Church Membership in Puritan New England (Princeton, 1969), 279-286; Beales, "The Half-Way Covenant and Religious Scrupulosity: The First Church of Dorchester, Massachusetts, as a Test Case," William and Mary Quarterly, 3d Ser., XXXI (1974), 474-475; Moran, "Religious Renewal, Puritan Tribalism, and the Family in Seventeenth-Century Milford, Connecticut," William and Mary Quarterly, 3d Ser., XXXVI (1979), 241, 245; Bonomi and Eisenstadt, "Church Adherence in the Eighteenth-Century British Colonies," William and Mary Quarterly, 3d Ser., XXXIX (1982), passim.

31. Hosmer, ed., Winthrop's Journal, I, 282-283; Thomas, ed., Diary of Samuel Sewall, I, 267; Boyer and Nissenbaum, Salem Possessed, 204.

32. Cotton Mather, Pillars of Salt (Boston, 1699),

77; _Sibley's Harvard Graduates_, IV, 470; John
White, _The Gospel Treasure in Earthen Vessels_
(Boston, 1725), 37; Ford, ed., _Diary of Cotton
Mather_, I, 76.

Chapter Three

Beyond Tribalism

The extent to which Puritan ministers were "tribal," that is devoted exclusively to church members
and their children, is another crucial factor in determining whether New England was a collective Puritan
culture or a pluralistic society moving in other directions. For if preachers were not converting New Englanders to Puritanism, surely they turned to other
traditions and ideologies for guidance. Since Morgan
published The Puritan Family in 1944, historians have
accepted his argument that "New England ministers
actually did devote their energy primarily to the
'children of the church,' not to the outside world."
Even social historians today deem Morgan's thesis one
of his "most important discoveries," chiding him only
for failing to push tribalism to "its conceptual and
descriptive limits." One notable exception is Richard
F. Lovelace, a church historian, who in The American
Pietism of Cotton Mather traces the evangelicalism of
the Great Awakening back "through Mather to such
diverse exponents of Puritan spirituality as John
Cotton and Thomas Shepard." Ironically, given the
Revisionist emphasis on the "striking unanimity of
opinion not only among the body of settlers but also
among [the] secular and theological leadership" of
early Massachusetts, Morgan's interpretation has posed
the greatest challenge to viewing New England in terms
of a collective culture.1

Morgan built his case on ministerial rhetoric in
tracts and especially sermons, as did Lovelace, but
neither scholar carefully researched pastoral behavior. To be sure, ministerial actions, as already
shown, reveal a Puritan clergy devoted to serving
church members; indeed, such activities are an im-
plicit--usually explicit--requirement of any group of
pastors employed by particular congregations. But as
previously documented in the pastoral care for the
sick and the poor, Puritan divines were not, as Gerald
F. Moran and Maris A. Vinovskis found in their comparative approach to tribalism, "unusually loyal to
the families of the church." Moreover, the daily
attempts of ministers to convert all New Englanders
lend credibility to Lovelace's interpretation of Puritan literature as evangelical in outreach. For example, dozens of eulogies applaud ministers, like

Benjamin Wadsworth of Boston, for "watering the Seed sown in his public Preaching, by private dealing with Souls, and more direct Applications to Families and Persons." Ministers achieved such evangelism by going "abroad till candle-Light," as did Thomas Prince, who was always "ready to warn them that are unruly, to comfort the feeble-minded, and resolve the doubting Believer." In rural areas parsons traveled from farm to farm. For example, Samuel Phillips rode to each Andover home once a year with his wife behind him on the horse. Samuel Whiting of Lynn, who engaged "his Neighbours with no Discourse but what should be grave, and wise, and profitable," stormed taverns with the gospel, declaring to happy patrons: "Friends, If you are sure that your Sins are pardoned, you may be wisely merry." The censure not only quieted the group but allegedly "had a great Effect afterwards upon some of the Company." Moreover, ministers welcomed callers --whether travelers, transients, or townspeople--into their parsonages, testifying with "obliging Courtesy" about "holy Religion unto them." Thomas Symmes of Bradford even summoned townsfolk to his home and thereby was "Eminently Skilful . . . in Private Application to Souls." By such "Christian Conference" some pastors reputedly "did more Good, than some Abler Preachers in the Pulpit." Thus, elderly preachers with waning pulpit skills sometimes dedicated themselves more fervently to "Private Visits."[2]

If Morgan's tribalism thesis was not so firmly entrenched among historians, as well as the impression that ministers were in their libraries not the streets, we could drop the matter with these eulogistic tributes and conclude that ministerial evangelism nurtured collective culture in Puritan New England. But reversing conventional wisdom requires much documentation, and Cotton Mather's frequent and varied efforts to convert New Englanders supplies it. Mather regularly visited Bostonians in their homes, seeking to change each from a "great Sinner" to a "true Convert." On one occasion he told a man: "Well the God of Heaven hath by His Word been calling you; expect now to have Him speak unto you by a Blow!" A few days later the man fell from the top of a house and received "a Blow, whereof hee lay, for some weeks, as dead." Upon recovery, he reflected on Mather's prophesy and quickly joined Willard's South Church. Another time Mather halted Ferdinando Turyl, a "poor carnal sorry Old man," right in the street and said: "How d' ye do, Old Man! I am glad for to see you

44

still in this World; I pray God, prepare you for another! I suppose it won't be long before you are
called away; Can I do you no Service!" A shaken
Turyl came the next day to Mather, who instructed him
on "how to prepare for Death" and gave him Grace Triumphant and "a Peece of Money." Mather continued to
meet with Turyl until he died seven weeks later. At
his funeral, Mather learned from Turyl's friends that
he had undergone a "wonderful Change," constantly
praying and reading Grace Triumphant, a "continual
Companion," and seemingly dying "a regenerate Man."
Reflecting on this, Mather noted that God had often
"strangely stirred" him to employ "very particular
Methods" to entice strangers into "His Covenant," who
subsequently died with "great Symptoms of Regenera-
tion." Even his barber finally succumbed to Mather's
relentless "Dropping of Counsils" and joined the North
Church. So did many of his servants, including one
who came to him a "wild, vain, airy Girl" but left
"disposed unto serious Religion."[3]

Mather was less successful with others, but he
nonetheless tried to convert them. He witnessed
twenty-three years to an "infidel Jew" at Boston,
periodically discussing theology with the man, writing
to him, and sending him The Faith of the Fathers and
La Fe del Christiano. But all to no avail, for the
Jewish fellow eventually moved to Jamaica where he
reputedly died "a hardened wretch." Reasoning that
nobody knew "whether the Glorious God may not send
some of His Elect" among sailors, Mather walked the
wharves, conversing with seafarers about Christ and
putting "Books of Piety in their Hands." He also
used "exquisite Methods of Insinuation" to engage
British soldiers in "Thoughts of Piety" and called
upon Boston "Watchmen, to spend their Time in devout
Exercises." And on trips to other towns, where Mather
had "private Opportunities to entertain and edify"
New Englanders, he inevitably recommended the "Service of Christ" to his traveling companions. Mather
himself best summed up the scope of Puritan evangelism
when he wrote: "Ardent my Cries, that the Spirit of
God may be poured out upon all flesh."[4]

Bits of scattered evidence indicate that the
claims of eulogists were accurate and Mather's actions representative. Hugh Peter preached to seamen
"aboard the Hector," a ship docked at Natascott, and
"kept the sabbath with them." Years later, an ex-
plosion injured several sailors aboard a ship that

had just arrived from Virginia, and Increase Mather hurried to the scene and tended the hapless victims. The following day Mather prayed with the dying captain, one Scarlet, and five "sorely wounded" seamen. The first priority of John Cotton, Jr., when he became the pastor of Plymouth, was to take his Ruling Elder and canvass the entire town, inquiring "into the State of Souls, and according as they found Frames either of the Children of the Church or others, so they applied Counsels, Admonitions, Exhortations and Encouragements." Such evangelism multiplied conversions, for his congregation grew rapidly during Cotton's first year and increased over the next twenty-eight. Likewise, Thomas Symmes, who took "great Delight" in his studies, was another whose evangelistic efforts were a "remarkable Success," almost trebling the size of his church in seventeen years. Though the town of Bradford had but 120 families, in 1720 Symmes admitted fifty-nine people to the "Sacrament, and 46 of them in three Months time, and 25 in one Day." At South Andover, more populous than the original center of the town, Samuel Phillips had to call on at least ten households a week to bring, as he did eventually, all his townsfolk into a collective culture rooted in their baptismal covenants. Rowland Cotton of Sandwich even proselytized Quakers, the most recalcitrant of New England sects, being thus "both loved and feared" by them. Indeed, the exception was the seemingly tribal John White of Gloucester, who once quipped: "I have not ordinarily fished for souls with a net, but with an angling rod."[5]

Likewise, pastors actually did invite into their parsonages all sorts of people in order to imbue them with Puritanism. Most often such visitors were townsfolk. James Noyes of Stonington "shewed himself even more than a Father" on such occasions. "While we sat at his feet," reminisced Eliphalet Adams about his youthful visits to Noyes's home, "how frankly would he Communicate his Advice and long Experience. How mightily would he Encourage us in our great Lord & Masters Work!" Cotton Mather had as many as a hundred townspeople gather at his house for "Prayers and Psalms and a Repetition of the Sermons preached in the Day." Pastors even boarded residents, if such an action promoted a Puritan New England. Samuel Cheever of Marblehead, for example, took in Josiah Cotton, the new schoolmaster, because he "was raw and young, not 19 years old, and therefore . . . gave way too much to that extravagance, Intemperance, Negligence

46

in Religion, and Disorderliness," that Cheever thought "too rife" at Marblehead. Preachers welcomed strangers, too, as when a dozen or more gave "very handsome Entertainment" to John Dunton, an English book peddler who toured New England in 1686. "The Civilities I receiv'd from him," Dunton wrote of Samuel Willard, "might (had I any Gratitude) engage me further to write his Character; but he's too great a man for me to Attempt it." And because of their commitment to spreading Puritanism internationally, several ministers ended up lodging regicides. When William Goffe and Edward Whalley, judges of the High Court who signed the death warrant of Charles I, fled to New England in 1660, they first stayed at Cambridge with Jonathan Mitchel, who treated them with "hospitality and friendship, and admitted [them] to the Lord's Supper and to private meetings for devotion." After seven months, however, pressures from the Crown forced Governor John Endicott to send the fugitives to New Haven, where John Davenport housed them until April of 1661. Then Thomas Kellond and Thomas Kirk, zealous royalists from England, drove the regicides completely underground for almost three years; hidden and sustained by laymen, they even spent two months in a cave near New Haven. Finally, in October 1664, John Russell of Hadley smuggled them into his parsonage. Subsequently, William Hooke of Taunton raised enough funds from New Englanders to help Russell support the fugitives until Whalley died in 1675 and Goffe in 1679. Such cooperation between ministers and laymen reveals a cultural web in New England devoted to nourishing Puritanism.[6]

There is even some evidence to suggest that Morgan overstated his case about the tribal character of Puritan sermons. The evangelical preaching of Thomas Hooker, which Morgan called a "magnificent exception," was to be heard from other pulpits. The famed Jonathan Edwards described William Williams of Hatfield as "eminently an evengelical Preacher." At Northampton Solomon Stoddard delivered sermons to "awaken secure Sinners, direct Souls about the great Work of Conversion, and to help Persons to judge of their spiritual State." Consequently his "Harvests" in 1679, 1683, 1696, 1712, and 1718 attracted so many converts, according to the Boston News-Letter, "as to give a happy Occasion for that admiring Question, Who are these that flie as a Cloud, and as the Doves to their Windows." Similarly, the preaching of Samuel Phillips at Rowley added ninety-three people to the church--fifty-four of them during revivals in 1669, 1684, 1685, and 1695. Such numerous conversions, resulting from pulpit evangelism and clerical visitation among the unchurched, offer much documentation for collective culture, as well as Lovelace's tracing of eighteenth-century revivalism to Puritanism.[7]

So do the clergy's dealings with criminals, for numerous pastors were like John Wilson of Boston who used "gracious Admonitions and Exhortations" to make them "remarkably penitent." One story, perhaps apocryphal, has Thomas Hooker trying to convert a petty thief, whom Hooker caught in the act of stealing his last piece of pork. "You ought to leave a part for me," Hooker reputedly declared, whereupon the man fell to his knees and begged forgiveness. Hooker then divided the pork with the intruder and sent him home a "conscience-scourged and repentant man." While it is doubtful ministers were that generous or the wayward that penitent, there is some truth in many cases to both points. Preachers did enquire "into the Condition of poor Prisoners," furnish them with clothes and other necessities, and counsel them about closing with Christ. And certain offenders seemed genuinely interested in the gospel, such as one who cried out to Mather Byles of the Hollis Street Church at Boston: "Can you think there are any hopes of me?" Sometimes when a prisoner was "very Penitent, and in wonderful Distress," pastors like Cotton Mather sought a pardon or reprieve for the offender that he might be "brought home to God, on this woful Occasion." Mather found that even a temporary stay of execution, as he secured in one case, could have "a strangely happy Consequence on the Soul of the Malefactor."[8]

But whether or not offenders were always enthusiastic, ministers vigorously evangelized them, as when Cotton Mather relentlessly pursued one Joseph, a black man sentenced to death for murder. Mather began by commenting on Joseph's sad condition but quickly moved to Christ's compassion. Then, reminding Joseph how "few times the Clock is to Strike" before his execution, Mather drove home the hideousness of murder. "What must you think," continued Mather, "that you deserve at the Hands of the Glorious GOD, whom you have so affronted and offended?"
Jos.   Be sure, I deserve to dy . . . .
Min.   Are you sensible . . . That unless you
         Turn and Live to GOD, it had been Good

```
Jos.    for you that you had never been born?
Min.    Yes, I am, Sir.
        But except there be more than your own
        Endeavour . . . Except GOD . . . Quicken
        you it will never be done.
Jos.    I say so, Sir.
Min.    But are you not Unworthy that GOD should
        Quicken you?
Jos.    I cast myself on His Mercy.
Min.    But . . . He may Justly withold the Help
        of His Grace from you. Tho' if you seek
        Him for it; there is Hope . . . .
Jos.    Yes, Sir, I know it.
```

Mather next launched into an involved explanation
about the righteousness of Christ, finally exhorting
Joseph to plead: "Lord, I am a Perishing Sinner. I
want a CHRIST." After Joseph acquiesced, Mather noted
five signs to identify hypocrisy. Weary of hairsplit-
ting, Joseph asked Mather to pray. Instead, Mather
pressed him about "Special sins," but Joseph's vague
answers led Mather to ask: "Is there any more that I
may do for you?" "No Sir; I can desire no more,"
Joseph replied. Although Joseph was black, Mather's
approach was typical of ministerial dialogues with
prisoners. Believing that God sprinkled the elect
among many nations, pastors advised criminals without
respect to race or, as apparent in other cases, sex.
"Who can tell," reasoned Mather, "but some Wretches,
by running into Prison, may run into the Arms of
Christ, and His victorious Grace!"[9]

Even on the way to the gallows pastors urged condemned prisoners to confess their sins and seek salvation through Christ. For example, when Joseph
Quasson, an Indian sentenced to be executed for murder, trudged to the scaffold, "most of the Ministers
of the County, and several others," accompanied him
on the "Mile's Walk," directing, encouraging, and
cautioning the prisoner. More commonly only one
preacher escorted the doomed criminal. The subsequent
portions of a touching dialogue that Mather Byles had
with twenty-seven-year-old Rebekah Chamblit, who was
executed at Boston for murdering her bastard child,
demonstrate that ministers tried to save the lost
until almost the moment of their death:

```
Minister.   Fear not . . . God is infinitely
            ready to pardon you . . .
Prisoner.   Alas, I've been a dreadful Sinner.
Minister.   And yet, what should hinder that
            you should not hope for a pardon?
```

	. . . Hear what the blessed Saviour says, Mat. IX, 13. <u>I came not to call the righteous, but SINNERS to repentance</u> . . . .
Prisoner.	. . . . <u>All I fear is the second Death</u>.
Minister.	. . . . What is it to believe on JESUS CHRIST? . . .
Prisoner.	<u>Faith in JESUS CHRIST is a saving Grace, whereby we receive, and rest upon Him alone for salvation</u> . . . .
Minister.	. . . . Lift up your eyes, and see the place [the gallows] . . . . lift up your eyes to GOD for his SPIRIT to help you . . . .
Prisoner.	<u>Lord JESUS, am I coming to this</u>!-- <u>Lord, whither am I going</u>!
Minister.	O remember the love of that SAVIOUR, who was executed as a Malefactor . . . [to] purchase eternal glories for you.
Prisoner.	<u>Lord JESUS, pity me</u>!

The poor woman, as she neared the gallows, grew "dis-ordered and faint." Byles continued to utter short words of encouragement to her until they arrived at the execution site. Perhaps his final words paral-leled those spoken by Cotton Mather to James Morgan, another condemned murderer: "Oh that I might meet you at the Right Hand of the Lord Jesus in the Last Day . . . . The Great God, who is a great Forgiver, grant thee Repentance unto Life . . . . With Him, and with His free, rich, marvellous Infinite Grace, I leave you. <u>Farewell</u>." Thus, despite their reputation for the strict enforcement of New England law and ex-ploiting the public punishment of criminals for "moral tales," in these and other cases ministers also hoped to win souls for Christ in an on-going effort to keep New England Puritan.[10]

Evangelism rather than tribalism also typified the clergy's activities among blacks, native Ameri-cans, the denizens of other colonies, and their on-going program of Protestant world missions. As early as 1641, according to John Winthrop, a "negro maid, servant to Mr. Stoughton of Dorchester, being well approved by divers years' experience, for sound knowl-edge and true godliness, was received into the church and baptized." John Eliot, who lamented that "the <u>English</u> used their <u>Negro's</u> but as their <u>Horses</u> or their <u>Oxen</u>," exhorted all slaveholders to instruct their blacks in Christianity, chiding masters for thinking "God made so many thousands of reasonable creatures for nothing but to serve the lusts of epicures or the gains of manonists." Such pleas failing, Eliot proposed to catechize blacks himself, if their masters "would send their Negro's once a Week unto him," but he did not "live to make much Progress in this Undertaking."[11]

By 1700 there were about 1000 blacks in New England, and most lived in seaports like Boston or Newport, Rhode Island. Thus, in 1693 Cotton Mather organized a Society of Negroes which met at his house on Sabbath evenings. Within a year other ministers rallied to support that Society, and twenty-five years later Mather was still summoning "a Number of black Sheep" for prayer and instruction. In 1716 Mather decided to establish a charity school for blacks. Because he subsidized this school at his "own single Expense for many years," it outlasted charity schools for poor whites and thus earned him the scorn of hostile racists. "A Lieutenant of a Man of War," wrote Mather, "has called his Negro-Slave by the Name of COTTON-MATHER" so that he could "assert Crimes as committed by one of that Name, which the Hearers take to be me." Nonetheless, Mather continued instructing blacks "in Reading the Scriptures, and learning their Catechism." At Newport, one of the chief slave marts in America, Congregationalist Nathaniel Clap also cared for the "precious Souls" of bondsmen and schools them in the way to "Inherit Eternal Life." While as late as 1776 a majority of the blacks in New England were still unconverted, more had become Christians, if only nominally, than in plantation colonies. Therefore, on the basis of "comparative analysis," as called for by Moran and Vinovskis, it appears Puritans were less tribal about converting blacks than southerners. It follows, too, that New England must have been more united--embedded in collective culture--than colonies in the South.[12]

Unfortunately, a comparative analysis of Puritan efforts to convert native Americans with similar labors by clergymen in other regions is hindered by the absence of studies about the latter. But the sweeping assertion by historian William Kellaway that the New England Way was "basically antipathetic to evangelical endeavour" can be judged qualitatively, assessing particular missionaries, and quantitatively, measuring how many ministers attempted to convert

Stanley Library
Ferrum College

112761

native Americans. As to qualitative evidence, the
work of dedicated missionaries among native Americans
has already been carefully documented by historians--
ironically by Kellaway himself and by Alden T. Vaughan.
The unceasing efforts of John Eliot, the "Apostle to
the Indians," and later John Eliot, Jr., described by
his father as a "good workman in the vineyard of
Christ, my assistant in the Indian work, a staffe to
my age," immediately come to mind. So do the labors
of the Mayhews on Martha's Vineyard, spanning from the
initial work of Governor Thomas Mayhew and his son,
Thomas, Jr., in the 1640's to the peripatetic Experience Mayhew's "prudential Care and Oversight of five
or six Indian Assemblies" on the Vineyard from 1694
until 1758. Less renowned pastors also toiled faithfully among the native Americans. Samuel Treat of
Eastham, for instance, "imparted the Gospel" regularly to over 500 adult Indians in his township and
instructed four Indian preachers at his home once a
week. Similar evidence documents the Indian missionary work of John Wilson, John Cotton, Jr., Daniel
Goodkin, Jr., Peter Thacher, Roland Cotton, Joseph
Gerrish, Samuel Danforth, Jr., Samuel Whitman, Joseph
Baxter, Josiah Torrey, and Josiah Cotton.[13]

   Quantitative analysis, untapped by historians of
Indian missions, also suggests that too little has
been claimed about the missionary zeal of Puritan
ministers. Consider the fact that thirty-two of 531
preachers--about 6% of the ministry--became missionaries. One out of seventeen is a significant number
but how significant? If compared to the number of
prolific publishers among ministers--twenty-seven or
about 5% of the clergy--it is obvious that clergymen
were more committed to Christianizing native Americans
outside their tribe than publishing treatises for
church members. Moreover, there were many preachers--
impossible to count accurately--like Thomas Shepard,
Benjamin Colman, and all of the Mather dynasty that
assisted missionaries whenever possible. They occasionally preached to native Americans, wrote pamphlets
for them, raised funds for missionary work and "poor
Indians," and served as Commissioners for the Propagation of the Gospel. In 1718 Cotton Mather expanded
his charity school for blacks to include native Americans in order to convert them. Ministers tried to
rally laymen, too, as when eleven Boston ministers
reminded parishioners that "the Churches of the Reformation have done so little for the Propagation of a
Faith" among Indians. All this evangelistic work by

1675 had at least nominally converted approximately 23% of the native population. Only comparative studies can determine the full significance of that percentage, but clearly it calls the notion of Puritan tribalism into question and documents that even some native Americans fostered collective culture in New England.[14]

Another long overlooked indication of collective culture in the Puritan colonies is the evangelical efforts of ministers to spread Puritanism throughout the Americas and other parts of the world, for it is unlikely that Puritans would have sent workers and charity to such regions unless their homefront was well-secured. Thus, as early as 1642, the New England clergy heeded a plea from Virginians in Nansemond County for a "supply of faithful ministers," sending William Tompson of Braintree, John Knowles of Water-town, and Thomas James, a New Haven minister, to Virginia for the "advancement of the Kingdom of Christ in those parts." Nor did these ministers introduce Virginians to Puritan tribalism, for they "preached openly unto the people for some good space of time, and also from house to house exhorted the people dayly." Even after the governor and other "malignant spirits" in 1643 forced Tompson and Knowles to return to Massachusetts and drove Thomas James to England, New Englanders continued to promote Puritanism in Virginia, exhorting the Nansemond brethren to per-severe and not emigrate to Bermuda. About five years later, John Cotton, who was "ever shewing of Kindness to Somebody or other," succored Nathaniel Whyte and a little band of nonconformists in the Bahamas. His generosity and solicitous fund raising, according to Cotton Mather, turned out to be a "most memorable Story," for there was "no Man who did exceed, and but one Man who did equal, this Devisor of Liberal Things, in that Contribution." Although this donation of £700 reached those "poor People" on the day they divided the last of their food, such relief eventually proved inadequate because the islands were too barren to sustain a flourishing plantation.[15]

This first-generation commitment to missionary work outside New England was not nonpareil. Every generation had ministers willing to leave New England to establish and nurture little bands of Congrega-tionalists in the Middle and Southern Colonies. After resigning his post at Plymouth in 1697, John Cotton, Jr., helped found a church at Charles Town, South

Carolina, and faithfully shepherded that flock. He
catechized, preached a lecture once a fortnight, held
private meetings and public fasts, made frequent
visits to the sick, opposed gainsayers, counseled
doubters, and hence became "the instrument of edify-
ing and quickening many saints and converting many
sinners." In fact, soon after his arrival he baptized many converts, admitting twenty-five of them to
full communion. Although yellow-fever ended Cotton's
life six months after his founding of the Charles Town
congregation, Hugh Adams and Joseph Lord, New England
ministers who had fathered churches at Wandoe River
and Dorchester respectively, carried on Cotton's work.
In addition to Virginia and South Carolina, Puritan
ministers held forth in many other places. To cite
but a few examples, Jeremiah Hobart, Joshua Hobart,
and George Phillips preached in Long Island churches,
where by 1660 there were eleven Puritan settlements;
John Harriman, Jeremiah Peck, and Joseph Smith accepted posts in New Jersey; Nathaniel Bowers labored
two years at Rye, New York; and James Parker and
Solomon Stoddard ventured as far as Barbados. As is
often the case with missionaries, many of these
preachers served only a few years, or perhaps a
decade, before returning to a New England pulpit.[16]

Other ministers, though they never ventured beyond New England, supported missionary work from the
home front. Babette M. Levy's study of Puritanism in
the Southern and Island Colonies rightly concluded
that the Cottons, Mathers, and Winthrops were concerned with "the fate of any struggling Puritan
church, no matter how far from Boston." In response
to these "far-flung brethren," she observed, the
prosperous churches of Massachusetts sent practical
advice, material support, and "more than occasionally
ministers." Benjamin Colman was one of "many good
Men" doing whatever he could to propagate the "Gospel
into such Places as have been hitherto negligent or
averse to the Settlement of it." He collected money
for "the Maintenance of sutable Missionaries," giving
liberally from his own pocket. Cotton Mather also
raised funds for missionaries, even appealing to nonconformist ministers in England to support "their excellent Brethren who are conflicting with extreme
Difficulties, in our southern Colonies." Furthermore,
Mather recruited ministers to "labour for Christ in
any Field that shall be assign'd" and secured them
for specific posts, like the English garrison at
Annapolis, Maryland. He also wrote letters to

"eminent Persons" in the West Indies and to Sir William Ashurst in the British Parliament to promote the conversion of island blacks. Likewise, his letters and gifts to August Hermann Francke, the leader of Lutheran Pietism in Halle, Germany, and to Bartholomew Ziegenbalg and John Grundler, German missionaries at Tranquebar, India, reveal a deep commitment to world missions. To advance Puritanism among Eastern Indians, Mather composed and sent a proselytizing essay in Latin to a Catholic missionary. "If the French Priest . . . might be brought over to the Protestant Religion," reasoned Mather, "it would be a wonderful Service to the Countrey." In sum, Mather's missionary work reached at least into Rhode Island, New York, New Jersey, Maryland, the Carolinas, the West Indies, the Spanish Americas, Germany, France, and India. Of course, we always know more of Mather's efforts, because he left so many records, but he was not atypical. Indeed, what eulogists wrote about Benjamin Wadsworth characterized many New England preachers: "Yea, His Heart was much engag'd in sending the Gospel to dark Places, destitute of so great a Blessing; and he employ'd an active Hand, in that excellent Work."[17]

All this evangelism--the work among unchurched New Englanders, blacks, Indians, the populations of the Middle and Southern Colonies, and those of foreign lands--justifies revision of Morgan's tribalism thesis. To be sure, ministers did put their own congregations first; as Samuel Bache, a merchant, wrote of John Wilson: "So bountiful to all: But if the Poor/Was Christian too, all's Money went, and more,/His Coat, Rug, Blanket, Gloves; he thought their due/Was all his Money, Garments, one of two." But ministers also unceasingly aided and witnessed to those outside the tribe and supported missionaries venturing beyond New England. Perhaps the greatest impact came from what might be called English tribalism. "Native Americans were required to become like Europeans," explained James P. Rhonda, "in all aspects of life--in matters of sex, marriage, economy, and government, as well as religion. The Indian who embraced Christianity was compelled, in effect, to commit cultural suicide." Thus, when Puritans failed to convert large numbers of people, whether Indians, Africans, Spanish Americans, or Frenchmen, it resulted more from this insistence upon "cultural revolution," that is, full participation in a collective culture, than any failure to spread the gospel. Moreover, the actual evangelical labor of ministers establishes, as Lovelace surmised from sermons, the "Puritan roots of the American phase of the Great Awakening."[18]

In sum, Puritan evangelism demonstrates that ministers were not intellectuals isolated from mass culture. Preachers brought the gospel to people wherever they were to be found: on the streets and wharves, in homes, barracks, ships, taverns, prisons, slave quarters, Indian villages, and sometimes mission fields. Even Cotton Mather, who published endlessly, regularly haunted such places seeking converts. Moreover, pastors made their parsonages a "Bethesda, for the Hospitable Entertainment" of churched and unchurched. Again, though Cotton Mather had "Be Short" inscribed above his study door, he "never seemed to be in a Hurry." "He would say some good and suitable things to every one that came to Him," wrote Thomas Prince. And Mather's diary entries about counseling at home confirm Prince's rhetoric, as when Mather invited widows and orphans to share his "Table once a Week; and oftner, if they please" or boarded such persons gratis, if necessary, to make his "House to become an Home" for the needy. And he resolved never to take even a "Dish of Tea" with such callers or boarders without "pursuing some holy Intention." Finally, considering the many individual converts that Puritan evangelists made and the scattered revivals they fostered, it is apparent that ministers had a steady influence on the course of New England culture. While preachers failed to win everyone in their quest for a Puritan New England, they did keep Puritanism a vital influence on the minds and lives of many people in the region.[19]

Notes

1. Morgan, <u>The Puritan Family</u>, 175; Gerald F. Moran
   and Maris A. Vinovskis, "The Puritan Family and
   Religion: A Critical Reappraisal," <u>William and
   Mary Quarterly</u>, 3d Ser., XXXIX (1982), 32; Lovelace, <u>The American Pietism of Cotton Mather:
   Origins of American Evangelicalism</u> (Grand Rapids,
   1979), 283; McGiffert, "American Puritan Studies
   in the 1960's," 41.

2. Moran and Vinovskis, "The Puritan Family and Religion: A Critical Reappraisal," 33; Thomas Foxcroft, <u>Elisha Lamenting After the God of Elijah</u>
   (Boston, 1737), 61; <u>Sibley's Harvard Graduates</u>,
   V, 349, 435; Joseph Sewall, <u>The Duty, Character
   and Reward of Christ's Faithful Servants</u> (Boston,
   1758), 15; Mather, <u>Magnalia</u>, Book III, 159-160,
   IV, 142, III, 50; Ford, ed., <u>Diary of Cotton
   Mather</u>, II, 75-76; John Brown, <u>Divine Help Im-
   plored</u> (Boston, 1726), 69.

3. Ford, ed., <u>Diary of Cotton Mather</u>, II, 472, I, 12,
   372-373, 346, II, 257-258.

4. <u>Ibid.</u>, I, 300, II, 500, 741, 458, 555, 86, 606,
   I, 232, II, 449.

5. Hosmer, ed., <u>Winthrop's Journal</u>, I, 182; Green,
   ed., "Diary of Increase Mather," 344; <u>Sibley's
   Harvard Graduates</u>, I, 498-499, V, 435, III, 324,
   IV, 422; Brown, <u>Divine Help Implored</u>, 69, 37.

6. Adams, <u>Eminently Good and Useful Men</u>, 43-44;
   Ford, ed., <u>Diary of Cotton Mather</u>, I, 131; Sib-
   ley's Harvard Graduates, IV, 400, I, 113-115,150;
   "John Dunton's Letters from New England," Prince
   Society, <u>Publications</u>, IV (1867), 75-76; Thomas
   Hutchinson, <u>The History of the Colony and Province
   of Massachusetts-Bay</u> (Cambridge, Mass., 1936 edi-
   tion), I, 183-187; John Davenport to William
   Goodwin, September 2, 1665; Edward Collins to
   William Goffe and Edward Whalley, June 1, 1672,
   M.H.S., <u>Collections</u>, 4th Ser., VIII, 127, 134-135.

7. Morgan, <u>The Puritan Family</u>, 175; <u>Sibley's Harvard
   Graduates</u>, III, 263, II, 113, I, 226.

8. Mather, <u>Magnalia</u>, Book III, 50; Samuel Frank
   Child, <u>The Colonial Parson of New England: A</u>

Picture (New York, 1896), 146; Ford, ed., _Diary of Cotton Mather_, II, 237, 337, 93, 244, 458; John Webb, _The Greatness of Sin_ (Boston, 1734), appendix.

9. Cotton Mather, _Tremenda_ (Boston, 1721), 31-40; Ford, ed., _Diary of Cotton Mather_, I, 272.

10. Samuel Moody, _A Summary Account of the Life and Death of Joseph Quasson_ (Boston, 1726), 24; Thomas Foxcroft, _Lessons of Caution_ (Boston, 1733), 64-68; Mather, _Pillars of Salt_, 83; Richard Slotkin, "Narratives of Negro Crime in New England, 1675-1800," _American Quarterly_, XXV (1964), 3-4.

11. Hosmer, _Winthrop's Journal_, II, 26; Mather, _Magnalia_, Book III, 207.

12. Francis J. Bremer, _The Puritan Experiment: New England Society from Bradford to Edwards_ (New York, 1976), 205; Ford, ed., _Diary of Cotton Mather_, I, 176-177, II, 532, 379, 500, 663, 706, 442; Lorenzo Johnson Greene, _The Negro in Colonial New England, 1620-1776_ (New York, 1942), 264-267, 285, 289; John Callendar, _A Discourse Occasioned by the Death of the Reverend Mr. Nathaniel Clap_ (Newport, 1746), 30, 32; Moran and Vinovskis, "The Puritan Family and Religion," 33-34.

13. Kellaway, _The New England Company, 1649-1776: Missionary Society to the American Indians_ (London, 1961), 5, 120, 81-121, 228, 276; Vaughan, _New England Frontier: Puritans and Indians, 1620-1675_ (Boston, 1965), 245, 235-308; [Thomas Prince], _Some Account_ appended to Experience Mayhew, _Indian Converts_ (London, 1727), 306, 299; _Sibley's Harvard Graduates_, II, 305, 279, III, 324-325, 245, IV, 316, 148-151, 420, 401; J. Franklin Jameson, ed., _Johnson's Wonder-Working Providence, 1628-1651_ (New York, 1937), 263-264; Mather, _The Comfortable Chambers_, 26; Grindal Rawson and Samuel Danforth, "Account of an Indian Visitation, A.D. 1698," M.H.S., _Collections_, 1st Ser., X, 129-134.

14. Selement, "Publication and the Puritan Minister," _William and Mary Quarterly_, 223-224; Ford, ed., _Diary of Cotton Mather_, II, 240, 442, 500;

Mayhew, Indian Converts, preface; Bremer, The Puritan Experiment, 202.

15. Hosmer, ed., Winthrop's Journal, II, 73-74, 351-353; Jameson, ed., Johnson's Wonder-Working Providence, 265; Mather, Magnalia, Book III, 28.

16. Sibley's Harvard Graduates, I, 503, II, 112, IV, 101-103, 322-323; Babette M. Levy, "Early Puritanism in the Southern and Island Colonies," American Antiquarian Society, Proceedings, LXX (1960), 265-267, 293, 297; Douglas Edward Leach, The Northern Colonial Frontier, 1607-1763 (New York, 1966), 51; Frederick Lewis Weis, The Colonial Clergy and the Colonial Churches of New England (Lancaster, Mass., 1936), passim.

17. Levy, "Early Puritanism," 89; Turell, The Life and Character of the Reverend Benjamin Colman, D.D., 75, 69-70; Ford, ed., Diary of Cotton Mather, II, 148, 198, 96, I, 570-571, II, 554, 576, 473, 771, I, 594-595, 315, 401, II, 84, 74, 665, 520; Cotton Mather, India Christiana (Boston, 1721), 62-87; Ernst Benz, "Pietist and Puritan Sources of Early Protestant World Missions (Cotton Mather and A. H. Franke)," Church History, XX (1951), 28-55; Joseph Sewall, When the Godly Cease and the Faithful Fail (Boston, 1737), 29.

18. Mather, Magnalia, Book II, 44; Ronda, "'We Are As Well As We Are': An Indian Critique of Seventeenth-Century Christian Missions," William and Mary Quarterly, 3d Ser., XXIV (1977), 66-67; Lovelace, The American Pietism of Cotton Mather, 283.

19. Sibley's Harvard Graduates, II, 485; Kenneth B. Murdock, ed., Selections from Cotton Mather (New York, 1926), xxvi; Prince, The Departure of Elijah Lamented (Boston, 1728), 20; Ford, ed., Diary of Cotton Mather, II, 65, 349, 440, 78.

Chapter Four

New England and the New England Mind

No factor is more important in determining the
degree of collective culture in New England than the
influence of ministerial literature upon the lives of
ordinary people. If ministers penned scholarly tomes
for intellectual colleagues and European peers, it is
unlikely such erudite books appealed to commoners or
greatly influenced their mundane lives. If, however,
the clergy published works "responding to colonial
needs," then the "world of print in seventeenth-century New England bespeaks collective mentality."
Focusing on the writings of Cotton Mather and those
inspired by the Antinomian Controversy, David D. Hall
concluded the latter, deeming such publications to be
"in harmony with the modes of collective mentality."
More recently, I found that 69% of all ministerial
publications were popular homilies and another 10%
were devotional-instructional treatises of the same
ilk. My statistics led Youngs to conclude: "the very
affinity between the printed word, the spoken word,
and the New England congregation lends credibility to
Miller's belief that society and intellect were
closely related."[1]

Puritan divines certainly thought their writings
were "intrinsic to a collective mentality they shared
with ordinary people," sometimes announcing their
purpose for publishing was to mold lay opinion and
mass culture. John Cotton called printed sermons
"clusters of ripe grapes passing under the press" to
benefit all nations. Samuel Moody of York, Maine,
similarly wrote that "both Hearing and Reading are
Means of Divine Appointment for the Conversion of
GOD's Elect, and building up the Church of CHRIST in
Knowledge, Faith and Holiness." Moody even deemed
the printed word superior, declaring that published
sermons could be studied and thus "more fully understood . . . for, if, in Hearing the Word, we understand it not, the Devil is ready to catch away the
precious Seed." Similarly, Increase Mather printed
books for people "in remoter Parts of the Country,
who never had any Opportunity to hear me Speaking in
the Name of the Lord." And that elite ministers
allowed for the literacy level of commoners is apparent in a request George Curwin of Salem made to Benjamin Wadsworth about publishing a tract on baptism.

"He desired," recalled Wadsworth, "that what should be written might be adapted to the Capacity of the meanest; and might be Short also, that so it might be the more easily bought, and charitably distributed, where it might probably do good." Equally sensitive to lay ability, Thomas Shepard stopped elaborating on the Trinity in Certain Select Cases Resolved (1648) when he feared having "waded too far in this divinity, the clear knowledge of which is reserved for us in heaven." This emphasis on reaching the widest possible audience fostered the ministers' "plain style," a literary genre and preaching mode that Murdock over thirty years ago argued brought Puritanism to "simple people." Such commoners appreciated and embraced these clerical writings, too, as can be seen in the laity's "repeated Requests" for ministers to publish sermons that met with "great Acceptance in the Country." To be sure, some clerical publications "Smelt of the Lamp" and were the "Result of many Years serious Enquiry after the Truth," but few, if any, were beyond the comprehension of literate New Englanders.[2]

But what of the illiterate? Lockridge argued these "peasants"--about 70% of the women and 40% of the men--were not privy to the world of print and transmitted knowledge orally. David D. Hall considers Lockridge's statistics "suspect," implying rates were probably higher, but recent data on early Cambridge, where 23% of the women and 64% of the men were literate, confirms Lockridge's estimates of literacy. Hall is right, however, to posit that literacy rates do not "really define the relationship between colonists and the world of print," because a "common language linked all social groups." Still another factor, which both Lockridge and Hall overlooked, is that literate people read and witnessed to the illiterate. Historians have long known that laymen took notes on sermons and read or expounded on them at home to their families. For example, by her "husband's speaking" Martha Collins of Cambridge, Massachusetts, saw her "original corruption and miserable condition and so had a hungering after means which were most searching." All it took, then, was one literate spouse to expose a whole family, one pious parishioner to enlighten his neighbors, one innkeeper or a patron to read to a curious crowd, one captain or seaman to inform an entire crew, and one penitent criminal with the skill to read to other prisoners. Lockridge's emphasis on face-to-face communication, and there is evidence in Thomas Shepard's "Confessions" and elsewhere that it was widespread, thus ironically turns out to support Hall's claim that "colonists lived easily in the world of print."[3]

The extent of this transmission of ideas to laymen through ministerial literature becomes clear when examining the clergy's book distribution, as Cotton Mather wrote about it: "an incredible deal of good may be done by distributing little books of piety." In fact, over the generations ministers did use this strategy to reach out to all New Englanders--literate and illiterate, rich and poor, churched and unchurched --and occasionally to people in other regions and nations. Certainly the reading or recommendation of a tract by a captain or crew member to a fellow seaman did not typically have as much impact as when a teenager, like Betty Sewall, repeatedly studied one to the point of being "terrified." Yet, mariner John Trumbull reported: "coming to sea by some men checking me there . . . . I thought I would learn to read it again. And reading Poor Man's Pathway, they told me the more I read the more I would delight in it but I read in it only to learn to read . . . . then reading book of repentance, learning some sins yet I lived in, so saw my misery." Such cases reveal that Puritan literature did reach laymen, edify them in varying degrees, and foster collective mentality in New England.[4]

Unfortunately, little evidence remains that first-generation ministers personally handed out tracts, especially in the early decades when they were busily erecting their "City upon a Hill." This is largely because their diaries were spiritual autobiographies that traced their long and arduous path to grace and sanctification rather than records of their daily activities. But we do know that the founders usually published treatises to enlighten and edify laymen, including those arcane works by John Cotton and Richard Mather on the "Ecclesiastical Constitution of the Country." Moreover, certain ministers, like Hooker, Shepard, and Eliot, shouldered less of the burden of consociation and hence specialized in "Composures of a more Practical sort." In 1641, for example, Shepard published The Saint's Jewel (1641) to "reap its due fruit from those whose hearts are rightly affected." Thus, there is no reason to doubt that ministers, as Peter Gay argued, "brought books with them on the immigrant ships, imported books from Europe as soon as they had settled, circulated their precious volumes among their friends, and disposed of them in their wills." Nor is it unlikely that the clergy passed out their own publications to promote the New England Way or resolve "Cases of Conscience."[5]

There is proof that after mid-century, when churches were well-established, towns prospering, and the presses at Cambridge and Boston in full swing, the founders personally distributed tracts. John Eliot wrote and circulated several unpublished catechisms that were "more particularly designed as an Antidote for his own People, against the Contagion of such Errors as might threaten any peculiar Danger to them." He also passed out Indian translations of English texts, including a logic primer, grammar, creed, catechism, and the Bible, to convert and edify native Americans. In 1686 Eliot gave John Dunton, an Englishman visiting New England, two dozen books to hand out in England to promote Indian missions. At Stamford, Connecticut, John Bishop circulated a treatise by Increase Mather on eschatology, while John Higginson of Salem distributed Mather's book on "Prayer & the Sacraments." Higginson, the author of four tracts, dispensed his own works, too, as when he exchanged books with Samuel Sewall in the winter of 1697. Moreover, the patriarchs encouraged younger colleagues to continue this tradition. After receiving in 1682 a copy of Increase's sermon about the "sore persecution of the Saints in France," Cobbett informed Mather that "Jesus will one day . . . graciously recompense what you have done" and thanked him for sending "very many other books." First-generation preachers, therefore, put Puritan literature into the hands of the people, striving thereby to mold a collective New England mind.[6]

As dissenters grew in number, the New England Way splintered into rival camps, and ties with Britain weakened, second-generation ministers relied even more on distributing tracts to preserve collective culture in New England. Increase Mather is a prime example. Besides giving treatises to Bishop, Higginson, and Cobbett, he sent them to Simon Bradstreet of New London, one of several towns in western Connecticut that acted as "safety valves for the dissenters from the Puritan colonies." To combat the Baptists, who with others had driven Bradstreet to rail against that "cursed Bratt Toleration," Mather forwarded treatises such as The Divine Right of Infant-Baptisme (1680). Finding those effective with New Londoners, Bradstreet asked Mather to write and distribute "some elucubra-

tions" defending Sabbatarianism. "I am apt to think,"
Bradstreet lamented, "among good christians there is
not one in a hundred able to maintain the Xtian Sabbath with any great strength . . . an idle sophister
would drive them, & run them into a hundred absurdi-
ties." Two years later when Bradstreet received an
almanac (written by young Cotton Mather) and several
other books from the elder Mather, he declared: "I
am your great debtor upon these accounts." Increase
also handed out tracts at Boston, where there were
many alternatives to Puritanism. His A Brief Discourse (1686), which denounced the Book of Common
Prayer and kissing the Bible when taking an oath, was
distributed free in the streets of Boston that "this
Lamp of the Sanctuary then may give Light unto the
whole House." To keep the eschatology of laymen like
Samuel Sewall orthodox, Mather gave them his A Dissertation Concerning the Future Conversion of the Jewish
Nation (1709). And to gain the support of English
Puritans, as well as participate in international
Protestantism, Mather sent numerous pamphlets to such
Nonconformists as Jane and William Hooke, Thomas
Jollie, Samuel Petto, Jonathan Tuckney, Samuel Baker,
and Samuel Cradock. Mather succeeded, too. "This I
am sure of," Jane Hooke wrote after receiving Mather's
A Brief History of the War with the Indians (1676),
"we forget you not in our prayers at the throne of
grace." In fact, Joshua Churchill felt slighted until
he too received three books from Mather: "I have
often wondered when letters & bookes have been sent
to my brethren, I could not be favoured with any."
Author of 104 different works, Mather undoubtedly
distributed tracts on every topic about which he
wrote, for he published such works that they "might
be Preached A Second Time in the way of the Press."[7]

Mather and Bradstreet were not the only second-
generation ministers dispersing tracts to shore up
the New England Way. James Fitch of Norwich, Connecticut, handed out Mather's tracts and copies of his own
publications. In 1681, Fitch sent Bradstreet a manu-
script--"three sheets of paper, well filled by a dex-
terous & able hand to prove the change" to Sunday--to
counter New London Anabaptists. Two years later Fitch
undoubtedly distributed his A Brief Discourse Proving
that the First Day of the Week is the Christian Sabbath (1683), probably an elaboration on his earlier
manuscript. At Ipswich Thomas Cobbett circulated Ne
Sutor ultra Crepidam (1681), a tract written by
Samuel Willard in "answer to the late Absurd &

scandalous narrative of John Russel and his Anabaptisticall crew in Boston." Although few, if any, Baptists troubled Cobbett's parishioners, he feared that with the "toleration of Antipedobaptists in the generall, here in New England, as they are in Old, they might soone flock over hither thereupon so many as would sinke our small vessel; whereas in that greater ship of England, there is no such danger."[8]

To influence orthodox New Englanders regarding church polity, second-generation ministers handed out works to advance their respective views. In 1678 John Cotton, Jr., appealed to Increase Mather to send Thomas Thornton of Yarmouth copies of The First Principles (1675), and A Discourse Concerning the Subject of Baptisme (1675), two of Mather's tracts which Thornton hoped would win laymen to the half-way covenant. "There are 5 or 6 dissenting bretheren," Cotton explained to Mather when requesting twenty copies of the "11th principles & de Bap . . . to establish the unsettled" at Yarmouth. Though Cotton neglected to mention why he needed fifteen extra copies, Robert G. Pope suggests Cotton gave them to similar dissenters in his own Plymouth congregation. While there is no extant proof, it seems likely John Davenport and Nicholas Street, colleagues at New Haven, passed out Another Essay for the Investigation of the Truth (1663), a work opposing the half-way covenant, to counter those promoting the innovation. The use of similar methods by rival ministers would account in part for the rise in differing mentalities among laymen, for surely pastors won some parishioners by handing them a pamphlet and face-to-face explaining and recommending its contents to them. Jonathan Mitchell recognized the potential impact of such an approach when he wrote about the publication of Shepard's The Parable of the Ten Virgins (1660): "let it be a welcome providence to have these truths . . . put into your hands . . . . Get them into your houses to read, nay, into your hearts to feed upon, as a choice and precious treasure."[9]

By Cotton Mather's time, preachers encountered ever greater challenges to maintaining collective culture. New philosophies threatened orthodoxy. More dissenters demanded toleration. Merchants and lawyers further replaced ministers as community leaders. The British tightened imperial controls and thereby curtailed the legal power of Puritan leaders to stop these movements. Thus, to maintain

whatever grip they had on the laity, third-generation
ministers turned even more to "continually scattering
Books of Piety" among New Englanders, reminding them:
"Remember, that I am speaking to you, all the while
you have this Book before you!" Clearly, this state-
ment by Mather as well as his practice of distributing
"at least six hundred Books in a Year," indicates that
the clergy believed their literature influenced the
minds of laymen and advanced Puritanism in New England. Orthodox laymen thought so, too, for one reason they put up "Bills," or notes, in the North Church
which identified those bound for sea, fallen into
"some great Affliction," or recovered from sickness,
was to enable Mather to send "suitable Books" to such
needy and possibly receptive people.

A careful look at Cotton Mather's tract distribution, therefore, reveals both how deeply Puritan
literature penetrated the mentality of New Englanders
and how many trends it had to counter. Many of the
books Mather handed out promoted his brand of orthodoxy among young people. To families with children,
he gave Cares about the Nurseries (1702), Parental
Wishes and Charges (1705), or Good Lessons for Children (1706). Sometimes he promised a child a "Peece
of Money, for every one of the Lessons, that he learns
without Book."[10] Mather put The A,B,C, of Religion
(1713) in grammar schools to reinforce lessons learned
at home. And to indoctrinate French Protestant children at Boston, he supplied their instructor, Pierre
Daille, with Le Vrai Patron des Saines Paroles (1704),
a pamphlet to help them "learn the Language, and improve in Knowledge and Goodness." To students at
Harvard and Yale, he gave The Old Pathes Restored
(1711) to combat "Pelagian Encroachments"; Supplies
from the Tower of David (1708) to counter Catholicism,
Quakerism, socinianism, pelagianism, antinomianism,
anabaptism, and sabbatarianism; and The Christian
Philosopher (1720) to prove that new philosophies
were no enemy to Puritanism. When President John
Leverett, a latitudianarian, recommended that col-
legians read Anglican writers, Mather bombarded Harvard with books by English and European reformers to
"correct the present wretched Methods of Education."
He also gave undergraduates Golgotha (1713), a
"Lively Description of Death" to promote early piety,
and Honesta Parsimonia (1721) to "prevent that Great
Folly and Mischief, The Loss of Time." For adoles-
cents who took up a trade, Mather had A Good Master

67

Well-Served (1696) about the "Properties & Practices"
of a good apprentice.[11]

To influence adult members of his flock, Mather
distributed The Right Way to Shake off a Viper (1711)
about responding to malign criticism and Genethlia Pia
(1719) to guide their thoughts on a birthday. Pro-
tecting them from the "Mischief" of Baptists and
Quakers, he circulated Baptistes (1705) and Little
Flocks Guarded against Grievous Wolves (1691), respectively. Mather also attacked their vices in
Advice from the Watch Tower (1713), which warned
against evil customs and offered methods for their
prevention and suppression. The "WATCHMAN," as Mather
styled himself, used The Bonds of the Covenant (1709)
to save church members from the "Snares of a wretched
Formality" in religion and worship. "My Design," he
wrote, "is to lodge it in the Hands of all that have
offered Themselves unto the Covenant in my own Church,
or that shall do so."[12]

When they suffered afflictions, Mather gave books
to New Englanders both in and outside the tribe.
"Wanting a Book, to be lodg'd and left, with such as
are in sorrowful Circumstances," he wrote The Cure of
Sorrow (1709), which reveals how closely Puritan literature could be tied to the culture of the masses.
Nor was this a fluke, for after distributing all his
copies of The Cure of Sorrow, Mather published The
Obedient Sufferer (1718) as a replacement. He also
distributed Orphanotrophium (1711) to orphans, An
Essay to do Good unto the Widow (1718) to encourage
women who lost their spouse, and Advice from Taberah
(1711) to advise fire victims how to profit from "so
Calamitous a Desolation." To counter witchcraft,
Mather dispersed The Wonders of the Invisible World
(1693) and Unum Necessarium (1693), both including a
covenant for readers literally to sign. Mather furnished the poor, of whom he kept a catalogue, with
Bibles or his Pascentius (1714), which explained "How
to Live in Hard Times." With the sick, Mather left
Wholesome Words (1703) and A Letter About a Good Man-
agement under the Distemper of the Measles (1713).
And to pregnant women, he gave Elizabeth in her Holy
Retirement (1710). Unable to visit personally with
all the "many Scores of sick families," Mather engaged pious physicians, midwives, and "honest Men" to
spread Puritanism among the masses by distributing
books among the ill and the pregnant.[13]

Mather's evangelistic outreach through book distribution further documents his impact on popular culture. Living close to the waterfront, Mather would "Walk down on the Wharf, talk with the People of the Vessels, and lodge Books of Piety in their hands." He placed in "many . . . Vessels, a Bible for the use of the Ship's Company, with a Promise from the Captain, that there shall be a suitable Use made of it." In 1709 he published The Sailours Companion and arranged that naval officers in several ports would place "convenient Numbers of these Books, in every Vessel that clears and sails from them." Three years later he distributed The Fisher-mans Calling, which alerted crusty seadogs to the "Calls of their Saviour," through fishing merchants. During Queen Anne's War, Mather furnished both sailors and soldiers with A Golden Curb (1709) and Ye soldier told what he shall do (1707). To other prospective converts, he delivered Man Eating the Food of Angels (1710), A Family Sacrifice (1703), and A Soul Well-Anchored (1712), providing a "Quantity of Silver, in purchasing a Number of them, to disperse where they might be serviceable." For blacks, Mather resolved to place The Negro Christianized (1706) in "every Family of New England, which has a Negro in it." Mather even wrote Reasonable Religion (1700), which scholars since Miller have viewed as an erudite bench mark in the rise of New England rationalism, because he wanted "a little Book, to leave in the Families of my Neighbours, where I make pastoral Visits."[14]

Mather tried to make his views heard outside Boston and thus "scattered Books of Piety about the Countrey; yea, in all the Towns of these Colonies." En route to Andover in 1706, for example, he met children on the road and "bestowed some Instructions, with a little Book upon them." He often forwarded Bibles or Frontiers Well-Defended (1707) to "ungospellized Places" to fight "Irreligion and Profaneness and Disorder." Or to new settlements without ministers, such as Arrowsick and Brunswick, Maine, he sent Indians and Christians "Instruments of Piety, suited unto their Occasions." To certain southern colonies "infested with Antinomian Troublers," he dispatched Adversus Libertinos (1713) to establish the "Holy Law of the Glorious God, upon The Principles of Justification by the Faith of the Gospel." In New York, where the Church of England spread "Pelagian Errors," Mather circulated The Old Pathes Restored. To Marylanders endangered by "Delusions of Popery," he delivered The

Fall of Babylon (1707) by the hundreds. As far as the
Carolinas--perhaps to South Carolina to be redis-
tributed by French Huguenots--Mather scattered Man
Eating the Food of Angels, Memorials of Early Piety
(1711), and Bonifacius (1710).[15]

Like his father, Mather was internationally
minded, spreading his works "to serve the Designs of
Religion, in other Plantations. Yea, in England, in
Scotland, in Ireland, in Saxony." He forwarded many
tracts to England--at least twenty of which were
originally published by London printers and several
more reprinted there--and A Letter of Advice to the
Churches of the Non-conformists in the English Nation
(1700) reveals his polemical zeal and belief that
Massachusetts was a unified "New-English Israel" for
all the world to emulate. Mather also tried to protect Old Englanders from the Arianism popularized by
William Whiston, whose anti-Trinitarianism cost him a
Cambridge professorship in 1710. Thus, Mather furnished his contacts at the University of Glasgow, an
institution to which he had close ties, with literally
scores of his Christianity Demonstrated (1710) and
Things to be More Thought Upon (1713) for redistribution. Similarly, when in 1724 Mather thought Catholic
Frenchmen were "very near a mighty and a wondrous
Revolution," he sent Une grand Voix du Ciel a la
France (1725) to "instruct them in the only Terms,
which the Friends of a Reformation must unite upon,
and exhibit unto them an incontestible System of pure
and undefiled Religion." Mather also conveyed Faith
Encouraged (1718), a brief tract on the "strange Conversion" of some Jewish Children at Berlin, to "many
of the Jews in several Places and Countreys"; The
Negro Christianized to the "principal Inhabitants" of
the West Indies; India Christiana (1721) to Europeans
concerned with the "Glorious Design" of spreading
Puritanism throughout the world; and A Pastoral Letter
to the English Captives in Africa (1698) to prisoners
"under their terrible Calamities."[16]

Mather once wrote about his book distribution:
"Perhaps I overdo: no other Minister in the Land
would so do." He even considered quitting "this ex-
pensive Way of serving my flock." But he "check'd
this Thought," and after a widow he later visited
gave him forty rare books for his library, Mather concluded that the "Lord smiles" upon ministers who hand
out tracts. Despite Mather's tendency to inflate his
importance, the extant data support his claim. But

70

then no other minister left reams of correspondence
and a diary of over 1500 printed pages. And no other
ministerial diary focuses so richly on the daily work
of a pastor. But whether Mather was typical or not,
other third-generation preachers did hand out tracts
to shape public opinion. Peter Thacher, after forty-
five years in the ministry at Milton, still passed
out books, as when he gave "2 of Mr. Bailys allman-
acks" to Jeremiah Bumstead, an active member of the
Old South Church in Boston. Solomon Stoddard circulated The Doctrine of Instituted Churches (1700),
"strenuously promoting his position concerning that
right which persons sound in the doctrine of faith, &
of (as he calls it) a holy Conversation, have to full
Comunion." And his evangelism led him to distribute
A Guide to Christ (1714) and Question Whether God is
not Angry with the Country for doing so little towards
the Conversion of the Indians? (1723). In 1705, every
clergyman in New England must have been handing out
Mather's The Rules of a Visit (1705), for members of
a Boston reforming society sent two copies of the book
"into every Town in the Countrey," designating one for
the local minister and the other, having the"Inscrip-
tion, To be Lent," for the populace. Mather himself
gave numerous other tracts "unto all the Ministers
far and near" for redistribution. For example, when
in 1728 the number of widows "greatly multiplied" in
a neighboring community, he purchased several copies
of An Essay to do Good unto the Widow and anonymously
sent them to the minister of the town. Surely his
colleagues were as eager as their benefactor to advance the "Kingdom of Truth" by circulating such books
among their townspeople.17

Fourth- and fifth-generation ministers, who published almost as much as the three preceding generations combined, left more evidence of distributing
books to mold provincial New Englanders. As usual,
we know the most about the activities of Boston ministers and their associates in nearby towns. For example, Thomas Prince, William Cooper, Thomas Foxcroft,
John Webb, all of Boston, and old Peter Thacher of
Milton cooperated in the distribution of Cotton
Mather's The Minister (1722), a "Memorial of the
Methods" by which preachers could be "very serviceable" in their communities. They sent it to "all the
Ministers throughout the Countrey," each knowing "what
counties, (or parts of the Countrey,) he will chiefly
take for his province in the Dispersion." Benjamin
Colman also "generously bestowed Books of Piety." On

two separate occasions, he sent his The Faithful Ser-
vant in the Joy of His Lord (1740) to Governor William
Shirley, whose child had died. You "have now one
less Attachment to Earth, one more Argument for
Heaven," Colman wrote to Shirley. Moreover, Colman
had the rare opportunity of distributing works by
Richard Baxter, when Samuel Holder, a wealthy London
Nonconformist, sent him thirty-nine sets of that
English divine's writings "to destribute among our
Churches, which amounts to more than Five Hundred
Pounds in our Money." To reach those outside the
tribe or at the bottom of society, Colman in 1713
proposed that every New England church establish a
fund for dispersing "Bibles, Catechisms, and other
Instruments of Piety among the Poor, as any particu-
lar Churches may see Occasion." As he grew older,
Colman increased his book distributions, putting into
the laity's "Hands some of the Meditations they have
heard with Patience and Pleasure." After receiving
The Government and Improvement of Mirth (1707), John
Saffin of Boston wrote Colman a response that clearly
documents the impact of ministerial literature on one
New Englander:

> Sir, Your Tract of Holy Joy I doe so Prize
> That on its worth, I can't Hyperbolize.[18]

Throughout New England, provincial clergymen
followed the lead of their Boston peers. Nathaniel
Eells of Norwell rode "over the Bay Colony and its
neighbors on ecclesiastical business, equipped for
any emergency by a volume of nearly a hundred of his
sermons tucked under his arm." At Littleton, Benjamin
Shattuck in 1720 squelched a witchcraft scare by distributing "a leaf from the book of the Mathers," which
shows literature could be as influential as folklore.
Similarly, Joseph Baxter of Medfield loaned Joan
Ellis, a deaf, eighty-year-old widow, Cotton Mather's
Things for a Distress'd People to Think Upon (1696),
which included a "Relation, of no less than Seven
Miracles." While reading the work, she allegedly "had
her Hearing suddenly restored unto her." As a chap-
lain in Queen Anne's War, John Williams had less
dramatic results but nonetheless gave books to soldiers to convert and edify them. To counter "the
Wild of Antinomian Extravagance" at Exeter, New Hampshire, John Odlin requested Mather Byles to send his
"Sermons upon FAITH EVIDENCED BY WORKS, and despersed
them about the Town." Later, when his townspeople
"condemned" Byles's tract, Odlin published and

distributed his own Doing Righteousness (1742) as a
"double Vigilance to guard the Doctrines of Grace."
Further north at York, Maine, parson Moody and a
"good number of Visitants" furnished Joseph Quasson,
an Indian condemned to die for murdering a "Fellow-
Soldier and Kinsman," with a "Variety of the most
suitable Books." They too had some influence, for
Quasson was "peculiarly blessed" by Stoddard's A
Guide to Christ and two pamphlets by English Nonconformists: John Fox's Time, and the End of Time (1670)
and Stephen Charnock's Two Discourses (1699), essays
that dealt with man's enmity to God and the salvation
of sinners. Though "blessed," Quasson was not as im-
pressed with the printed word as Moody, as one ex-
change between them reveals:

    Pris.   I have had many Books, and have read
           much,--but I don't see that I'm a lot
           the better.
    Vis.   O, you must not leave off by all Means:
           The Life of your Soul depends on it.

In Southern New England, Azarish Mather of Old Say-
brook, Connecticut, distributed Cotton Mather's Bonifacius and "some other things" he expected to "prove
Instruments of good." At Newport, Rhode Island,
Nathaniel Clap, one of the few Congregationalists
holding forth in "the licentious Republic" or "sinke
hold of New England," as some Puritans called Rhode
Island, passed out "numberless" tracts. According to
John Callendar, a Baptist minister in Newport who
preached Clap's funeral sermon in the more ecumenical
days of the mid-eighteenth century, Clap incurred
"considerable Expence" scattering books to "awaken
the Careless and Secure, Comfort the Feeble-minded,
Succour the Tempted, Instruct the Ignorant, and
quicken, animate, and encourage all."[19]

    One of the most impressive proofs that ministe-
rial literature shaped mass culture is the laity's
distribution of books. As early as 1642, when Charles
de La Tour, the French governor of Nova Scotia, sent
his lieutenant and thirteen men to Boston, one of the
ruling elders of the First Church gave the Roman
Catholic officer a copy of Les Pseaumes de David
(1606) by Augustin Marlorat, a Huguenot commentator.
"They staid here about a week," Governor John Winthrop recorded in his journal, "and though they were
papists, yet they came to our church meeting; and the
lieutenant seemed to be much affected to find things
as he did." Decades later at Boston, Old North Church
deacons, while engaged in "Dispensations of Charity,"

continued this tradition by handing out Cotton
Mather's Pascentius to the local poor. Pious laymen
who were not church officers also dispersed pamphlets.
Edward Bromfield, a counsellor in the Massachusetts
General Court from 1703 to 1720, subsidized Cotton
Mather's An Advice to the Churches of the Faithful
(1702) and gave two copies of it to each member of the
Massachusetts and Connecticut legislatures, asking the
representatives to give one of the copies to their
hometown pastor. "It proved highly acceptable and
serviceable," Mather rejoiced, "and many Ministers
even had it read in their Several Congregacons." At
Portsmouth, New Hampshire, Samuel Penhallow, a prosperous merchant and treasurer of that northern province for twenty-six years, also scattered Mather's
treatises. And Samuel Sewall, sometimes subsidizing
publications, passed out literally hundreds of Puritan
tracts all over New England, as this entry in his
diary reveals: "I carried 2 Duz. Mr. Willard's Books
about swearing, to Mr. Phillips; Duz. to Buttolp;
Duz. to Eliott; Duz to Boon." Poorer and less influential laymen distributed tracts, too. Sometimes
ministers supplied them. Cotton Mather, for example,
gave 1000 copies of Family Religion (1705) to several
laymen, who lodged them with the "prayerless Families"
in their communities and sent a "Bundle to every Town
in all these Colonies, and unto some other Places."
The Boston Society To Suppress Disorders, which admitted members for their piety not wealth, combined
the resources of many laymen to "publish and scatter"
works throughout New England, such as Cotton Mather's
A Monitory Letter to them who Needlessly & Frequently
Absent Themselves from the Publick Worship of God
(1701). Members of congregations also pooled their
money to print and distribute books, as when the
Watertown flock showed their "respect to the labors
and memory of their deceased Pastor," Henry Gibbs, by
publishing his Godly Children their Parents Joy in
1727.[20]

The book distribution of clergy and laity--long
ignored by historians--has thus confirmed several
theses. It documents that ministers were not scholars
writing for elite colleagues but popular writers
striving to win commoners through sermonic publications. Cotton Mather put it well when he lamented
that the Roman Catholics "do in one Point condemn the
Protestants; for among Romanists, they don't burden
their Professors with any Parochial Incumbrances; but
among the Protestants, the very same Individual Man

must Preach, Catechize, Administer the Sacraments,
Visit the Afflicted, and manage all the parts of
Church-Discipline; and if any Books for the Service
of Religion, be written, Persons thus extreamly in-
cumbered must be the writers." It also shows preachers were not tribal, writing only for church members,
but evangelical in their distributions, reaching beyond the tribe to all townspeople, regardless of race
and class, and to the inhabitants of other towns,
colonies, and nations. Finally, it proves that Puritan literature reached the masses and influenced their
thinking, which is why Benjamin Wadsworth chose rather
"to press those practical Duties that were not dis-
puted, than spend his Time in spectulative Contro-
versies." To be sure, book distribution indicates
there was more to the New England mind than Puritanism, such as Quakerism, rationalism, and just plain
irreligion, but the pervasiveness of Puritan pamphlets
suggests that New England "realities" were not as far
from clerical rhetoric as some historians have
claimed. However qualified, there was collective
mentality in New England.[21]

Notes

1. Hall, "The World of Print and Collective Mentality in Seventeenth-Century New England," 174-175; Selement, "Publication and the Puritan Minister," 226-227; Youngs, "Perry Miller and the 'Buzzing Factuality' of Colonial New England," 14.

2. Hall, "The World of Print and Collective Mentality in Seventeenth-Century New England," 177; John Norton, The Orthodox Evangelist (London, 1654), preface; Samuel Moody, The Doleful State of the Damned (Boston, 1710), i-ii; Increase Mather, Several Sermons (Boston, 1715), viii; Benjamin Wadsworth, The Bonds of Baptism (Boston, 1717), preface; John A. Albro, ed., The Works of Thomas Shepard (Boston, 1853), I, 314; Kenneth B. Murdock, Literature & Theology in Colonial New England (Cambridge, Mass., 1949), 181; William Williams, The Duty of Parents (Boston, 1721), iv; Increase Mather, A Dying Legacy of a Minister (Boston, 1722), 1; Cotton Mather, Just Commemorations (Boston, [1715]), 34; Experience Mayhew, Grace Defended (Boston, 1744), ii.

3. Kenneth A. Lockridge, Literacy in Colonial New England: An Enquiry into the Social Context of Literacy in the Early Modern West (New York, 1974), 39; Hall, "The World of Print and Collective Mentality in Seventeenth-Century New England," 166, 173; George Selement and Bruce C. Woolley, eds., Thomas Shepard's "Confessions," Colonial Society of Massachusetts, Collections, LVIII (1981), 3, note 8, 130-131.

4. Levin, ed., Bonifacius, 77; Hall, "The World of Print," 174.

5. Mather, Magnalia, Book III, 21, 89, 65; Albro, ed., The Works of Thomas Shepard, 286; Gay, A Loss of Mastery: Puritan Historians in Colonial America (Berkeley, 1966), 23.

6. Mather, Magnalia, Book III, 187; "John Dunton's Letters from New England," 193; John Bishop to Increase Mather, June 3, 1683, John Higginson to Increase Mather, August 22, 1682, Thomas Cobbett to Increase Mather, September 12, 1678, M.H.S., Collections, 4th Ser., VIII, 309, 282, 293-294.

7. William G. McLoughlin, New England Dissent, 1630-1833, The Baptists and the Separation of Church and State (Cambridge, Mass., 1971), I, 10; Simon Bradstreet to Increase Mather, April 20, 1681, and April 24, 1683, Jane Hooke to Increase Mather, June 8, 1677, Joshua Churchill to Increase Mather, August 25, 1684, M.H.S., Collections, 4th Ser., VIII, 477-480, 261, 639; Thomas James Holmes, Increase Mather: A Bibliography of His Works (Cleveland, 1931), I, 48; [Increase Mather], A Brief Discourse [Cambridge, Mass., 1686], preface; Thomas, ed., Diary of Samuel Sewall, II, 995; Cotton Mather, Utilia (Boston, 1716), iv.

8. Simon Bradstreet to Increase Mather, April 20, 1681, Thomas Cobbett to Increase Mather, December 13, 1681, M.H.S., Collections, 4th Ser., VIII, 480, 477, 291-292.

9. John Cotton to Increase Mather, August 26, 1678, M.H.S., Collections, 4th Ser., VIII, 247; Pope, The Half-Way Covenant, 189, 46; Albro, ed., The Works of Thomas Shepard, II, 10.

10. Ford, ed., Diary of Cotton Mather, I, 359, 548, II, 108, I, 421, 518, II, 64. Unless otherwise indicated, the treatises cited in the subsequent paragraphs on Mather are his own.

11. Ibid., II, 216, 94, 82, 615, 610, 247, 348, 611, 616, 53; Samuel Eliot Morison, Harvard College in the Seventeenth Century (Cambridge, Mass., 1936), 505-506, 541-542.

12. Ford, ed., Diary of Cotton Mather, II, 141, 669, 697, I, 142, II, 209, 13.

13. Ibid., II, 20-21, 526, 58, 516-517, 118, I, 155-156, II, 156-157, 111, 113, 387, I, 445-446, II, 265, 270, 272, 618.

14. Ibid., II, 555, 85, 14, 135, 11, 42, I, 480, II, 147, I, 564-565, 360-361; Miller, The New England Mind: From Colony to Province, 420; James W. Jones, The Shattered Synthesis: New England Puritanism before the Great Awakening (New Haven, 1973), 89.

15. Ford, ed., Diary of Cotton Mather, II, 26, I,

566, 593, II, 336, 184, 60, 64-65, I, 594-595, II, 42.

16. Ibid., II, 27, I, 312, II, 53-54, 66, 191, 776, 503, I, 564-565, II, 619, I, 260; Miller, The New England Mind: From Colony to Province, 164.

17. Ford, ed., Diary of Cotton Mather, I, 368, 522-523, II, 87, 697; S. F. Haven, ed., "Diary of Jeremiah Bumstead of Boston, 1722-1727," New England Historical and Genealogical Register, XV (1861), 305; John Russell to Increase Mather, March 28, 1681, M.H.S., Collections, 4th Ser., VIII, 83.

18. Selement, "Publication and the Puritan Minister," 226-227, 232; Ford, ed., Diary of Cotton Mather, II, 684-685; Turell, The Life and Character of the Reverend Benjamin Colman, D.D., 182, 194, 113, 75; Benjamin Colman, A Dissertation on the Image of God (Boston, 1736), i; Caroline Hazard, ed., John Saffin His Book (1665-1708) (New York, 1928), 168.

19. Sibley's Harvard Graduates, IV, 470, V, 494; Ford, ed., Diary of Cotton Mather, I, 274-275, II, 87, 60; John Odlin, Doing Righteousness (Boston, 1742), preface; Moody, A Summary Account, 2, 9-10, 12-13; McLoughlin, New England Dissent, I, 8; Callender, A Discourse, 28-29.

20. Hosmer, ed., Winthrop's Journal, II, 85; Ford, ed., Diary of Cotton Mather, II, 388, I, 410-411, II, 34, I, 520, 429; Thomas, ed., Diary of Samuel Sewall, I, 495; Gibbs, Godly Children their Parents Joy (Boston, 1727), xi.

21. Mather, Magnalia, "A General Introduction," para. 5; Sewall, When the Godly Cease, 31; Robert G. Pope, "New England Versus the New England Mind: the Myth of Declension," Journal of Social History, III (1969-1970), 96.

Chapter Five

From a Puritan to Yankee Culture

The pastoral work, evangelical outreach, and book distribution of the clergy document their spreading of Puritanism throughout New England to form a collective culture in the region. This is not to suggest, however, that ministerial ideas permeated every dimension of life in the Puritan colonies, for social historians since Eggleston have rightly traced much of the social, political, and economic behavior of New Englanders to "pre-industrial traits, and, more generally . . . to simply Anglo-American traits." Indeed, as shown in each chapter, pastors were not concerned with instructing parishioners how to plow their fields or build their fences--unless, of course, such activities led to communal strife--but strove to mold the religious beliefs (doctrines) and moral behavior (piety) of New Englanders. To be sure, their ideology influenced the social, political, and economic views of the colonists, as did Anglo-American traditions carried from England, but universal devotion to the Puritan religion was the paramount goal of ministers. Nor does the collective culture fostered by the words and deeds of clergymen reveal anything about the demography of early New England, an area best explored through non-literary sources.[1]

But mundane concerns, albeit vital to understanding certain aspects of everyday life among ordinary people, are not the most critical factors for evaluating the collective culture of doctrine and piety that has occupied Puritan ministers and professional historians. More important are the changes wrought in New England society with the passage of time that weakened the Puritan grip on New England culture--the Puritan to Yankee metamorphosis. Defining fully the terms "Puritan" and "Yankee"--to say nothing of the Puritan to Yankee transition--is immensely complex. In 1970, McGiffert identified seven different definitions of just Puritanism, and scholars have added several more since his article to continue the "particular glory of Puritan studies . . . against the temptation to become precisionistic (which is to say, puritanical)" and maintain "a certain accommodating ineffability." Yet, for assessing the forces that dissolved collective culture in New England, it is sufficient to define Puritanism, as Miller did, as

"that point of view, that philosophy of life, that
code of values, which was carried to New England by
the first settlers in the early seventeenth century,"
including also his emphasis on the homogeneity of "the
first three generations in New England" who shared an
"almost unbroken allegiance to a unified body of
thought." The term "Yankee," therefore, represents
the forces of pluralism in New England marked "by
burgeoning heresies, imperfectly absorbed or exer-
cised, by unexpected shifts of sentiment and language,
by breakings-in of alien ideas." Thus, the Puritan
to Yankee process, whether viewed as "declension" or
"the more complex study of varied Puritan develop-
ment," involves the replacement of Puritan thought
and practice by Yankee ideas and behavior.[2]

Several historians have already traced various
aspects of this trend to secularization or modernization, as some of them label the change from Puritan
to Yankee. Focusing on ideology, Miller uncovered
slow and subtle philosophical shifts in the collective culture of New England, leading him to conclude
that the "original system of Puritanism survived
without any drastic alteration" until about 1720. Investigating social, political, and imperial develop-
ments, Richard S. Dunn in Puritans and Yankees described "New England's gradual transformation from
Puritan to Yankee" as a seventeenth-century event.
For Dunn, John Winthrop resided in a Bible Commonwealth where Puritans ruled; Winthrop, Jr., found
himself in a restoration world of cosmopolitan and
entrepreneural attitudes, and the third generation of
Fitz and Wait Winthrop lived in "an increasingly complex, confused, materialistic, self-seeking society."
By 1700, according to Dunn, the "secularization of
the New England conscience" had occurred. Exploring
the behavior of ordinary people at Boston, Rutman
dated the modernization of New England much earlier
than Miller or even Dunn, declaring that by 1640 Winthrop's ideal of "subordination of self in the interest of the community for the greater glory of the
deity . . . was a medieval dream, and it was not to
be." Individualism, materialism, a Franklinesque
morality, and the separation of sacred and secular
had already transformed Winthrop's "ideal of the
medieval community . . . into the reality of modern
society." Most recently, Paul R. Lucas has supported Rutman's view with data about the Connecticut
Valley, claiming that Miller's "portrait of a monolithic, 'close-knit, tightly controlled,'" seven-

teenth-century New England "reflects myth more than fact."[3]

The pastoral labors of Puritan divines sheds some light, but by no means the last word, on these complexities in the breakdown of collective culture in New England. Their daily care for laymen reveals, as Rutman and Lucas documented, that there were secular forces in New England from the outset; that these forces, as Dunn found, gradually increased with each generation until by the 1680's Yankees outnumbered Puritans; and, as Miller discovered, there was a shifting Puritan orthodoxy that constantly influenced these changing New Englanders until new philosophies, dissenting religions, and internal innovations finally overwhelmed it in the eighteenth century. In particular, the clergy's book distribution, catechizing, aid to education, witchcraft counseling, and reproving of the wayward confirm these patterns, albeit with certain qualifications.

First-generation ministers before mid-century pursued pastoral activities as if their communities were relatively homogeneous and locked into collective culture. The books they wrote and circulated were primarily either about "the Points of Church-Government then debated"--thirty-one of 144 were on church polity, vastly more than any other generation--or about "Cases of Conscience" that troubled pious immigrants. Of course, there were Antinomian, Baptist and unclassifiable dissenters, but they were usually, like Roger Williams or one Captain Partridge, loners who could be easily suppressed by the Puritan majority. Partridge, who maintained "divers points of antinomianism and familism," is an especially good example. John Cotton counseled the captain in 1645 and then reported to the magistrates that there was "good hope to reclaim him wholly." However, the magistrates--impatient with any dissent in their tightly knit community--required "a present renouncing of all" and, failing to get it, banished Partridge to Rhode Island. Though such "strictness was offensive to many," it demonstrates there was enough consensus in Massachusetts to enforce precise uniformity of opinion.[4]

Only in the well-known, if not shopworn, Antinomian Controversy did first-generation ministers and magistrates face such widespread opposition to Puritan orthodoxy that they had no choice but to employ long-term methods of recovering the dissenters and uniting their own ranks. For nearly two years the clergy preached against the antinomian "errors, and prac-tises that so much pestered the Countrey," and numer-ous authorities intermittently met both privately and publicly with Anne Hutchinson and her many followers. "We gave them free leave, with all lenity and pa-tience," John Winthrop recorded, "to lay downe what they could say for their Opinions, and answered them, from point to point, and then brought cleare argu-ments from evident Scriptures against them, and put them to answer us." At one such private conference, no fewer than nine preachers interrogated and rebuked the wayward Hutchinson. But she and her cohorts con-sistently refused to "yeeld to the truth." By the summer of 1637 the orthodox had closed ranks enough for the Massachusetts General Court to call the first synod ever held in New England, which met at Cambridge on August 30, 1637. After twenty-four days of de-liberation, the synod summarily condemned eighty-two antinomian opinions. Subsequently, the First Church of Boston excommunicated the incorrigible, and later the Massachusetts General Court banished them from the colony. To cement any remaining cracks in the New England Way, John Winthrop and John Cotton published partisan histories of the controversy.[5]

Though less salient and disruptive than dissen-ters, there were worldly people, too; "crafty and guileful Souls" Hooker called them, reproving them "sharply" and "with Fear, pulling them out of the Fire." Yet, they were few in number, for unlike sub-sequent generations there is comparatively little ministerial reference to struggling with them. And when "wickedness did grow and break forth," as when in 1642 Thomas Granger of Duxbury committed buggery with "a mare, a cow, two goats, five sheep, two calves and a turkey," Puritans had much less trouble punish-ing or even executing such offenders than they did reproving or banishing dissenters. Sinners, there-fore, before mid-century never hindered the founders from erecting their "City upon a Hill" and only oc-casionally distracted them from nurturing church-goers.[6]

The same was true of witches. Not only were they scarce--none appearing until 1645--but when they finally surfaced, ministers dominated the situation. For example, in 1648 Samuel Stone of Hartford, Con-necticut, took "great pains" with Mary Johnson, "the

Success of Which, was very desirable, and considerable." Johnson confessed to "Uncleanness with Men
and Devils" and was "very Penitent, both before and
at her Execution." That same year William Tompson of
Braintree brought H. Lake's wife, a convicted Dorchester witch, to "great penitency." Though she "utterly
denyed" being a witch, before her execution Lake "jus-
tifyed God for bringing her to that punishment: for
she had when a single woman played the harlot, and
being with Child used means to destroy the fruit of
her body to conceal her sin and shame." Obviously,
such isolated outcasts were no threat to the prevail-
ing collective mentality.[7]

Finally, because society was predominantly Puritan, the piety of laymen tended to "minimize clerical catechizing and maximize that of the family."
Nevertheless, John Fiske of Chelmsford did by the
"most laborious Catechising, endeavour to know the
State of his Flock" from the 1630's onward, and similar evidence documents that at least seven other
first-generation preachers catechized from the outset.
But such ministers were in the minority and catechized
to continue the clerical practices they used in Old
England as much as to correct either the negligence
of New England families or the influence of alien
ideas.

Likewise, founding ministers did not have to
assume the primary responsibility for ensuring that
the youth of New England received a godly education.
Thus, their efforts in that area tended to be limited
to raising funds for Harvard College and its "poor,
pious, and learned" students. For example, in 1644
Thomas Shepard, discovering that "for want of some
externall supplys, many are discouraged from sending
their children" to Harvard, proposed to the Commissioners of the United Colonies of New England that
"the fourth part of a bushell of Corne" be given
yearly by every able and willing family in New England
to help needy scholars. The Commissioners, and later
the General Courts of Massachusetts, Connecticut,
and New Haven, endorsed Shepard's recommendation and
raised a "substantial contribution."[8]

What clearly emerges from each of these pastoral
areas, then, is a Puritan clergy striving for and
usually bringing New Englanders to the orthodoxy of
the Bible commonwealth. But despite such communal
homogeneity, at every turn the faint beginnings of

83

secularization are apparent. Those cracks that Rutman and Lucas emphasized appear. Puritans built their city and lone dissenters infiltrated it to trumpet their heresies and advance pluralism. Ministers brought their saintly flocks to Massachusetts, and clever sinners slipped in to erode piety and, as John Cotton wryly commented, to make "nothing cheap in New England but Milk and Ministers." The devil's witches found their way, too; and preachers had to counsel them and warn others of Satan's snares. And while many families catechized their children and supported education, others did not, forcing pastors in the 1630's to begin assuming two other responsibilities to counter secularization and maintain orthodoxy. Though these changes did not alter all New England at the breakneck pace Rutman documented at Boston, the population of the region was changing faster than Winthrop's political world or the theological one of the clergy. As Dunn rightly observed about the latter, the Puritan crusade lost eventually because of its "tendency to ossify into a rigid new orthodoxy."[9]

As surviving first-generation and young second-generation ministers watched 1660 approach, the fissures in their collective culture widened in every area. Even if a majority of New Englanders were Puritans in 1660, and historians have not yet compiled such statistics, by the 1690's Puritans would clearly be in the minority. Seeing this trend, ministers began writing and distributing more tracts, such as John Norton's The Heart of New England Rent (1659), to refute the ever-growing number of Baptists and Quakers. Thomas Thacher, hearing of "any Books left by the Quakers in any Houses" at Weymouth, not only supplied the family with polemical books but expropriated "Venomous Pamphlets."[10]

Ministers employed numerous other techniques to keep New Englanders from the "Sink of all Errors." When Quakers convinced one Weymouth man that his Bible was "altogether useless," Thacher met him on the street and took him into "a Neighbour's House, and privately there Talked with him, and . . . recovered him from the Error of his Way." John Cotton, Jr., held tutorial sessions at Plymouth, assigning each man at the meeting "sundry Questions . . . to return Answers to out of the Scripture," a preventive strategy that "for divers Years" achieved "good Success." In 1662, Seaborn Cotton of Hampton, New Hampshire, resorted to vigilantism to "keep the

Wolves from his Sheep." Putting himself at the "Head of his Followers, with a Truncheon in his Hand," Cotton's Puritan mob forced Quaker Eliakin Wardel to flee to Salisbury. Moreover, until about 1680, Puritans also tried to preserve orthodoxy with their civil code, imprisoning, fining, whipping, maiming, banishing, and executing dissenters who threatened "Jericho's Walls" with their "stinking Vapour from Hell."[11]

But religious dissenters were not alone in battering the walls of Puritan culture. Worldly persons assaulted it with "plain Trespasses against the Rules of a Godly and a Sober, and a Righteous Life." Though such jeremiads overstated the trend to irreligion, it is clear from the rise in clerical reproof of evildoers that after 1650 New Englanders were less scrupulous than Robert G. Pope argued but not as far gone as Rutman claimed. While references to the disciplinary efforts of first-generation ministers are rare, reports of second-generation preachers, like James Noyes of Stonington, Connecticut, striking "awe into the boldest Offenders" are comparatively common. Certainly Joshua Moodey unnerved the worldly at Portsmouth, New Hampshire, for he had townsmen order in 1662 that "a cage be made, or some other means invented by the Selectmen, to punish such as sleepe or take tobacco on the Lord's day out of the meeting in the time of publique exercise." At Hingham Peter Hobart battled against "Pride, expressed in a Gaiety, and Bravery of Apparel," advising fops to "adorn their Souls" not bodies, and was a "faithful Reprover" of those who cursed. He chided Drunkards, too, deeming tippling "Sitting at Meat in an Idol's Temple." So did Increase Mather, who warned Bostonians in 1673: "There is more Wine drunk in this Town, then in most Towns of the same greatness in the Christian world." By 1675 Mather had watched how the "Love of drink" had turned one Negos of Boston from a "strict professor" to a "Lamentable object, crying out yt ye devill had power over him, e yt yr was no hope for him, yt God had forsaken him." Little wonder Samuel Danforth, who loved "Good Orders and Manners," spied on the Roxbury tavern from his study window, and when he saw "any Town-Dwellers tipling there, he would go over and chide them away." Social dancers worried ministers, too, and thus Increase Mather published An Arrow against Profane and Promiscuous Dancing (1684) to halt the practice. And worst of all there were the "plots of papists, Atheists, &c," which ministers from even

rural towns discussed with their Boston colleagues.
After mid-century, then, Puritans encountered a
"looser sort of people," as Higginson of Salem called
them in 1670. Their strategy with them, as Ross
Beales concluded about the impact of the half-way
covenant, was to "extend the church's influence to as
many members of the community as possible . . . that
virtually no member of the rising generation would be
excluded from the benefits of both church discipline
and the preaching of the gospel."[12]

For different reasons, other New Englanders
strayed from ministerial control and dabbled in
witchcraft. Or at least they acted strangely enough
to give that impression, for nearly eight times as
many trials for that crime were held between 1650 and
1662 than before mid-century. Even more revealing,
pastors no longer always had the status to sway the
court system, as secular authorities drifted from the
sacred. In 1656 John Norton of Boston failed to save
Anne Hibbins, wife of a local merchant, from the gallows. Hibbins "was hanged for a witch," Norton
lamented, "only for having more wit than her neighbors . . . she having . . . unhappily guessed that
two of her persecutors, whom she saw talking in the
street, were talking of her." Though Norton's impotence was atypical because ministers remained authorities on witchcraft throughout the 1680's, his failure
revealed briefly New England's gradual change in
leadership from preachers to lawyers and merchants,
a shift that eventually contributed heavily to the
dissolution of collective culture.[13]

Similarly, by 1660 fewer New Englanders heeded
ministerial exhortations to indoctrinate children
with Puritanism, and thus more pastors had to catechize "the rising generation, both in familyes &
churches." John Cotton, Jr., first taught youngsters
once a fortnight but later stepped up his catechizing
to "Sabbath Day Noons at the Meeting House, the Males
one Sabbath and the Females another successively."
Increase Mather not only catechized but summoned
children individually to "enquire into yir sple
estates &c." Moreover, he diversified his instruction,
sometimes reading from the Cabinet of Mirth (n.d.), a
book of songs, to stir the interest of young pupils.
Thus in 1665, when Charles Chauncy of Scituate routinely exhorted a colleague to "Catechise every
Lord's Day in the Afternoon, so as to go through the
Catechise once in a year," he recognized that

ministers had to shoulder more work to counter secularization. If they did not follow his "Directions," the ranks of dissenting religions and the unchurched would surely continue to grow and erode collective culture.[14]

In addition to catechizing, ministers not only continued to be "a Father to the Colledge" and its "Scholars eminently pregnant and pious" but about mid-century further broadened their efforts to promote godly education. For instance, John Eliot helped found a school at Roxbury in 1645, and thirty years later he promoted the construction of another one for the expanding town. In fact, on July 10, 1689, Eliot deeded seventy-five acres of land in trust to John Weld, John Gore, John Watson, and Samuel Gore, and their heirs, to maintain that school and school-master at Jamaica, or Pond Plain, for the "instructing of the children of that end of the town (together with such negroes or Indians as may . . . or shall come to said school)." Such schools, Eliot once declared, were the answer to "How the Miscarriages which were among us might be prevented."[15]

Despite all their pastoral tactics and labors, those who differed with the Puritans prospered, outnumbering them by 1690, if not a decade or two earlier, and changing the dominant culture of New England from Puritan to Yankee. Being Yankee of course involved ideological plurality, and as already shown about their book distribution, ministers after 1680 wrote and passed out numerous tracts against the ever-increasing number of Baptists, Quakers, Anglicans, Catholics, Jews, sabbatarians, pelagians, antinomians, socinians, arians, and followers of Enlightenment philosophies. This was no longer Puritan New England; Puritans were but one faction, albeit large and splintered, contending for dominance. Being Yankee meant tolerance, too, and together these minority religions formed a majority that with the help of the British government and the Church of England brought de facto freedom of religion to New England. William G. McLoughlin has rightly concluded: "The laws requiring uniformity of belief and conformity of worship remained unchanged after 1682, but they became dead letters--and perhaps they had been so for a decade before the General Court secretly admitted it to the King." Moreover, certain Puritans--led by Benjamin Colman--had themselves become Yankee enough to adopt a new "catholic spirit," which had "no affection to

sanguinary punishments" of dissenters. In 1696 Cotton
Mather sent a "Token of several peeces of Eight," to
John Emblen, a poor Baptist preacher in Boston, and
by 1718 Mather so fully embraced the catholic view
that he participated in Elisha Callender's ordination
at Boston's Baptist Church. Seven years later Nathaniel Appleton, another Boston preacher of "catholick
temper," went so far as to allow John Comer to join
the First Baptist Church of Boston and still maintain
his membership in Appleton's congregation. "He be-
haved himself," Comer wrote of Appleton, "the most
like a Christian of any of my friends at that time
upon this account." Such ministers had drifted far
from the "good old Puritans" who fined, whipped, and
banished dissenters.16

Faced with such Yankee dominance, preachers had
to rely exclusively on pastoral labors to stem the
tide to rival religions, protect their flocks from
proselytizing, and nurture Puritan culture. Besides
dispersing more tracts, like Cotton Mather's Little
Flocks Guarded against Grievous Wolves (1691), ministers spoke privately with endangered parishioners.
One story in particular illustrates how much New England culture had changed by 1700. When "some En-
chanted with Quakerism, did actually, and without
Metaphor, Spit in his Face," John Wade, minister of
South Berwick, Maine, from 1699 to 1703, summoned no
magistrate but "bore it, and with Prayer and Patience
Recovered them." Even oldtimers like Increase Mather
substituted persuasion for compulsion, as when in
1676 he wrote a letter to one fallen into "desperate
Heresy," including "errors respecting discipline,
sacrts, theyr cov^t . . . & these Arminian Heterodoxia
respecting Christ's dying for these Repbates." Mather
did not threaten legal action but humbly pleaded: "I
desire still to respect you, & earnestly to beseech
Christ to let you see your error." Public debates--
once suppressed by Puritan clergymen--also became increasingly popular among provincial ministers. John
Bulkley of Colchester, Connecticut, was one such
standard-bearer, debating Baptists at Lyme, Connnecti-
cut, on the "following Heads, viz. 1. 'Tis the Will
of God some Children should be Baptized. 2. That
Sprinkling (or pouring Water on them) is sufficient
for the Ends of Baptism. 3. That 'tis lawful for
People to have a Tax laid on them for the Support of
the Ministers of the Gospel." Such debates soon gave
rise to many references in Puritan hagiography about
the prowess of third-generation orators. For example,

Samuel Phillips wrote of Nicholas Noyes of Salem:
> WITH Quakers he did oft Dispute,
> And never fail'd them to Confute.

Win or lose, these pastoral approaches to influencing
laymen reflected the demise of collective culture New
England and the rise of "free individuals relying upon
their own judgment to create the city of God upon the
American hill."[17]

Many of these free individuals, however, wanted
New England to be a city for men, a place of creature
comforts, rather than a holy Zion. Therefore, provincial ministers more than ever became "Eagle-eyed
to discern the Approaches of Sin," styling themselves
"Watchmen" who sounded the "Calls of GOD aloud in the
Ears of impenitent Sinners." They corrected young
people, who now and then liked "a Frolick, a revelling
Feast, and Ball, which discovers their Corruption, and
has a Tendency to corrupt them yett more." Ministers
prodded idlers, whether apprentices neglecting God's
calling, whom Cotton Mather pressed to "serve their
Masters with all possible Fidelity"; elderly persons
whom he told to "improve their Leisure-time in doing
Abundance of Good"; or a "poor Drone" for whom Mather
sought employment. In contrast, Joseph Green rebuked
the Howards of Salem Village for beating their maid,
one Mabel Evens. Though Mrs. Howard claimed "she had
never struck her so much as she deserved," Green told
her "she had been cruel and ought to repent and confess her sin. And . . . that she and her husband had
reason to go mourning to ye grace for their cruelty
to a naughty servant." Pastors found still others in
"ruinous courses of Gaming" and counseled them with
"all possible Fervency and Compassion."[18]

Especially troublesome for the clergy to reform
were the ever-increasing number of drunkards. According to old Increase Mather, by 1712 Bostonians not
only drank more wine than "most Towns not greater than
this in the Christian World," as they had in 1673, but
now consumed more "Strong Drink" as well. To halt
"Tavern Haunting" at Stamford, Connecticut, John
Davenport relied on "zealous Testimony" against "Intemperance in Drink," but a pathetically desperate
Peter Thacher took his cane to tipplers who lingered
too late at the Middleborough ordinary. Likewise,
excessive drinking among the poor at Boston enraged
Ebenezer Pemberton of Old South Church. In May of
1710, when Boston profiteers exported 6000 bushels of
wheat during a grain shortage and provoked a near riot

among the poor, Pemberton told Samuel Sewall they "were not God's people but the Devil's people that wanted Corn." "There was Corn to be had," emoted Pemberton, if the rioters "had not impoverish's themselves by Rum." Pemberton was no callous skinflint; indeed, reputedly his "Charities were Great." But the constant trend to impiety--symbolized by widespread consumption of "demon" rum--frustrated Pemberton and drove him to such harsh words.[19]

Sexual offenders were on the rise, too, and equally difficult to reform. New Englanders discussed "Self-Pollution" enough for Cotton Mather to publish and distribute The Pure Nazarite, which warned against the dangers of masturbation, though he doubted the following conclusion of a Swiss preacher: "If the old Punishment of Stoning to Death were to be inflicted on the Criminals, the neighboring Mountains would not afford Stones enough to serve the Execution." As early as 1676, Increase Mather heard that one A., his wife, and one B., all of Salem, might be having a ménage á trois because they "lay all in one bed." Mather exhorted them to repent and avert a "greater Judgt hastned on ys place." Likewise, Cotton Mather reproved many either in "danger of being ruined, by an indiscreet Amour," "detestable Adulteries," or "Infection by the Daughter of Babylon." As to the latter, what could be more indicative of a Yankee New England than Boston's bordelloes? Perhaps the fact that Mather could not stop the "very great Resort of young men" to them. In 1712 he rallied the Boston Society for the Suppression of Disorders to prepare a list of "wicked Houses in the Town" and assigned "particular Methods and Agents, for the putting of a Check upon them." But a year later he still had that list and had added a catalogue of men who patronized "Women of a very debauched Character." Again, it was to no avail, for in 1714 Mather continued to wonder how to shut down "some very wicked Houses, that are Nests of much Impiety."[20]

None of these "Censurable Evils" were new to New England, but in provincial society they flourished, and ministers could only effectively deal with them privately by pastoral counsel and reproof. To be sure, there remained a supply of pious laymen. Thus, when in 1707 Theophilus Cotton, the unmarried minister of Pamet, committed a faux pas by escorting a woman to Boston, he returned to his parish to find that the "whole place was in an uproar." "They fear I have been Lewd & vain with her & with others, too," Cotton lamented. But for every case like this one, there are numerous others that portray the laity as indifferent to religion, like the man whom Cotton Mather futilely labored with for over twenty years "to recover him out of the Snares in which he is perishing." Moreover, in provincial New England certain people even mocked such pastoral efforts, causing ministers to rationalize that "some of those very Scorners may reap saving Benefit in that very Method, which now they ridicule."[21]

More churchgoers, even if Pope is right about the scrupulosity of some of them in the 1660's, by the 1680's reflected this secularization of New England. Cotton Mather reprimanded his niece with "effectual Admonitions" for her "Vanities and Fooleries," just as he scolded one "unhappy Youth" who "tho' a Pretender to Religion, yett will curse and swear." Others profaned the Sabbath. "Do not spend any Part of this holy Time in Vanity," Joseph Sewall of Boston futilely reminded Harvard students, "nor in the study of humane Learning." Similarly, Cotton Mather exhorted Laurent Vandenbosch, minister of Boston's French protestant families, to "awaken that People unto a greater Observation of the Lord's Day; by the Neglect whereof they had given too much Scandal." Some churchgoers slept during sermons, and Samuel Moody once yelled from his pulpit: "Fire, fire!" When the parishioners awoke to ask where the fire was, Moody roared: "In Hell, for sleepy sinners." Moody also publicly rebuked the wife of one of his wealthier York parishioners for strolling proudly into the meetinghouse in a new hooped dress. "Here she comes," he declared, "top and topgallant, rigged most beautifully, and sailing most majestically; but she has a leak that will sink her to hell!" Other "foolish and froward" people quibbled over seating arrangements, forcing Cotton Mather to use the "Methods of Prudence and Piety, to manage such Roots of Bitterness."[22]

Two cases in particular reveal the secularization of at least some church members. The first involves Kathrin Russel, a Boston widow who had an "unlawful Offspring" because of her "lewd Carriage towards diverse Men at sundry Times." When Cotton Mather proceeded with her excommunication from the North Church in 1718, Kathrin's father, an "old and great Professor of Religion," and "his foolish Family" not only treated Mather "very ill, and with a strange Malice and Revenge" but used "violent Wayes to sow Discord among the Neighbours, and the Peace of the Church." Similarly, in 1720 John Barnard met with intense retinency from Sarah Wescott, a Marblehead woman who gave birth to three illegitimate children before being excommunicated. At least twice after the birth of her third bastard, Barnard tried in vain to visit Wescott at her home, but Sarah, learning of his calls, complained that she was "hunted like a partridge upon the mountains." A week after the thwarted visits, Wescott finally met with Barnard, only to reject his biblical arguments and personal entreaties. According to the Marblehead church records, even at her official excommunication Wescott defied Barnard by walking out during the proceedings and ignoring his commands "in the Name of Jesus Christ to Stay." An upstaged Barnard simply remarked: "Let her go; no doubt She is not of us." Such delinquent saints, though rare among churchgoers, received more support and sympathy in Yankee than Puritan New England.[23]

Even orthodox ministers in provincial New England occasionally violated Puritan social and sexual mores. The case of Michael Wigglesworth's mesalliance, which broke the New England convention of marrying equals, provides an example of how Puritan traditions were giving way to the rising Yankee society. When his first wife died in 1659, Wigglesworth did not remarry. But in 1679 at the age of sixty-eight he decided to wed his seventeen-year-old serving maid, Martha Mudge, who was "one of obscure parentage, & not 20 years old, & of no Chch, nor so much as Baptised." Increase Mather implored Wigglesworth to consider the following six arguments against the unholy match: it would 1) be a "grief of hrt" to his relatives, 2) shorten his life because of the sexual duties required by I Corinthians 7:3, 3) blemish his reputation, 4) discredit all ministers, 5) violate II Corinthians 6:14 which commanded Christians not to be "unequally yoked with unbelievers," and 6) disobey I Timothy 3:11 which required women to be "temperate, faithful in all things." Mather also advised Wigglesworth to overcome temptation by putting the maiden out of his sight and looking "up to the Lord Jesus for supplies of grace." Unconvinced, Wigglesworth flouted New England custom and married the teenage girl, and that his ministerial critics accepted his decision and continued to promote his career is even more indicative of the secularization of New England.[24]

This trend was also apparent in the transition from familial to ministerial catechizing, which Yankee commercialism "set irrevocably in motion" during the 1660's, because by 1690 no provincial clergymen thought it "an abasement or abatement of his honor, to stoop unto this way of teaching." Eulogists routinely lauded ministers as catechists, as when Thomas Foxcroft of Boston praised Benjamin Wadsworth for taking "a tender Father's Pleasure" in catechizing "feeble Lambs." Moreover, ministers experimented with "sweet Variety" to discover the best method of indoctrination. Grindall Rawson of Mendon catechized his entire congregation on Sunday afternoons and taught smaller groups on weekdays. Thomas Symmes required the young men of Bradford to answer questions before the congregation, thereby "proposing Advantage to the whole Assembly." In contrast, Israel Loring of Sudbury avoided pushing neophytes "too hard," especially when dealing with people of "ill education." And Cotton Mather, always ready to "make one Experiment more," held sessions at his home, in the church, and occasionally at the Boston grammar school. Sometimes he selected "great Points of practical Piety" to focus on with a particular child, requiring "a great Attention from all the rest." Or he concentrated on "peculiar Vices" of the children and set "Charges agreeably upon them." In 1713, when a measles epidemic ravaged children, he reminded those of "restored Health" of the "Admonitions of Piety, suitable to the Occasion." Clearly provincial New Englanders, as Yankees pursuing wealth, had shifted the burden of catechizing youngsters to the clergy. And ministers, striving to impede further secularization, more defections to rival religions, and greater dissolution of collective culture, had to add that duty to their many other "Parochial Incumbrances."[25]

Secular schoolmasters, too, occasionally had "to be advised, about a good Conduct" and employing ministerial "Projections and Proposals for the Kingdome of GOD, in their Schools." As documented earlier, provincial ministers had to inundate Harvard students with Puritan books to counter the college's "wretched Methods of Education," namely Yankee latitudinarianism. To aid and personally influence poor but promising undergraduates, ministers continued the tradition of subsidizing those with "an uncommon Capacity for Learning." Moreover, in cosmopolitan Boston the clergy also established charity schools to promote the Puritan version of a "godly Education" among the

poor children of the city. Cotton Mather also set
one up for blacks and native Americans. In rural
areas pastors, like Joseph Green, saw to the erection
of schools for all the young people and made sure
teachers were orthodox. While these activities sprang
from clerical evangelism and charity, they were also
an attempt to reverse the modernization of New England
and reestablish Puritan culture.[26]

Just as the growth of dissenters and erosion of
Puritan ways indicate that the clergy lost control
over New Englanders, the laity's treatment of witches
and their victims reveals a similar decline in ministerial authority. But this blow came after 1690. Indeed, before then, as Richard H. Werking has argued,
ministers successfully countered secularization in
this area and kept "the spiritual world a reality by
reporting instances of witchcraft." Besides writing
and distributing books on the topic to "confound
atheists and inject religious zeal," they invited
laymen to watch them deliver victims "captivated by
the Evill one." In 1671 Willard held a "soleme day"
of prayer on several occasions not only to exorcise
Elizabeth Knapp, a Lancaster girl afflicted by
"Devills, in their hellish shapes," but to edify
onlookers. That Willard commanded the situation is
clear from the fact that, when Knapp accused a local
woman of witchcraft, Willard exonerated her by press-
ing Knapp until she made "2 evident & cleere mistakes."
Similarly, in 1688, when "hellish Witchcraft" tor-
tured the children of John Goodwin, a Boston mason,
several pastors assembled laymen at the "haunted
house" for prayer. And no doubt the ministers im-
pressed those onlookers, because "Immediately upon
this Day, the youngest of the four children was delivered." Goodwin himself declared: "their love and
pity was so great, their Prayers so earnest and constant, that I could not but admire at it." Moreover,
when a young man stopped to talk with Cotton Mather
about "curing the Atheism and Blasphemy which he complained his Thoughts were more than ordinarily then
infested with," Mather took the youth to see Martha
Goodwin who "was then molested with her unseen
Fiends." Such wonders of the invisible world, then,
were a strong antidote to what Mather called Sad-
duceeism and Atheism.[27]

Even at the outset of the Salem affair, ministers
were still holding their position as witchcraft authorities. Thomas Clark of Chelmsford exonerated a

local woman by convincing his townspeople that the spectral evidence against her was but a "design of Satan to render an innocent person suspected." Similarly, Samuel Phillips and Edward Payson, both ministers at Rowley, cleared Elizabeth How of Ipswich by allowing her to confront her young accuser and ask "whether she had ever done her any hurt." To which the child replied: "No, never; and, if I did complain of you in my fits, I knew not that I did so." At Boston, Cotton Mather held days of prayer and fasting for Mercy Short, an afflicted servant girl. And when Short accused several Laymen in the room of never praying "once in all their Lives," Mather chided her for the allegation and simply warned bystanders to repent if any did have the "guilt of a Prayerless Life."[28]

But as the hysteria over the Salem witches mounted, the loss of ministerial power in Yankee New England--so obvious in their inability to control dissenters or the worldly--began to gape in this last bastion of clerical authority. Secular judges, appointed by Governor Phips to the Court of Oyer and Terminer, became the final authorities on witchcraft, reflecting that New Englanders, as David Thomas Konig put it, had their "own secular ideology that led them . . . toward a legalistic prosecution of an extra-legal threat to society." Thus, civil authorities rejected Cotton Mather's offer to provide "Meat, Drink and Lodging for no less than Six of the Afflicted, that so an Experiment might be made, whether Prayer with Fasting" might not end the crisis "without giving the Civil Authority the trouble of prosecuting." Likewise, though John Hale promised Nathaniel Cary, a Charlestown shipbuilder, and his accused wife, Elizabeth, a private interview at the Salem parsonage, they ended up in the Salem alehouse where Elizabeth's accusers "all came in" and began "to tumble down like Swine." The local justices, who sat "in a Chamber near by, waiting for this," then issued a warrant for Elizabeth's arrest. The court also ignored faithful shepherds like Phillips and Payson, eventually condemning Goody How despite their earlier testimony about her innocence.[29]

In fact, except for John Hale, Samuel Parris, and Nicholas Noyes, who eventually joined the court in flouting clerical methods for combatting witchcraft, Puritan ministers ended up opposing court proceedings and decisions.[30] In April of 1692, Samuel

Willard and Joshua Moodey, both Boston preachers at
the time, went so far as to help two of the accused,
Philip English and his wife, escape from a Boston
jail. On June 15, several Boston ministers urged
Governor William Phips, his council, and the Court
of Oyer and Terminer, to prosecute vigorously proven
witches but raised serious caveats about spectral
evidence as a grounds for conviction. The devil,
they warned, could assume the shape of an innocent
person. Similarly, in August John Wise signed an
Ipswich petition that formally protested the conviction of John Proctor of Salem Village, the petition
declaring that God "sometimes may permit Sathan to
personate, dissemble, and thereby abuse innocents."
But not until nearly everyone in New England was un-
easy about the trials, because of too many convictions, did ministers regain respect and authority in
matters of witchcraft. Only then, in October of 1692,
could Increase Mather halt the convictions by denounc-
ing in a sermon--subsequently published as Cases of
Conscience--the court's reliance on spectral evidence.
Though ministers later blamed themselves for "not
appearing with Vigor enough to stop the proceedings
of the Judges," clerical impotence in the Salem
tragedy was but another symptom of the secularization
of New England.[31]

Over three generations, then, New England changed
from a predominantly Puritan to a predominantly Yankee
society. The pastoral labors of the clergy reveal
that by 1660 churchgoers were not catechizing their
children, by 1670 sinners were escaping punishment,
by 1680 dissenters were commanding toleration, and
by 1690 witchcraft cases were no cure for secularization. To be sure, this was all a matter of degree,
and historians will never be able to quantify the
exact pace of the disintegration of collective Puritan culture. Moreover, New England communities
ranged from stable, usually inland, agricultural
villages to rapidly changing commercial seaports on
the coast. The location and varying economies of
such towns, as Boyer and Nissenbaum have shown, often
determined the population's allegiance to Puritanism
or newer Yankee ways. Yet, there were "vagabond fel-
lows" in country parishes and pious laymen at Boston,
indicating that geography did not always determine
beliefs and practices. And historians to date have
been unable to quantify whether Puritanism lingered
longer in remote towns or in urban centers, although

many defer to Rutman's data and conclude Boston "was far advanced" along the path to secularization.[32]

Despite such caveats, it is clear from what today would be called the "case load" of Puritan ministers that the change from a Puritan to a Yankee culture in New England was a steady one--save in witchcraft cases. Decade after decade, pastors had to catechize more children, involve themselves more deeply in education, reprove more sinners, and combat more dissenters. Only in witchcraft, which rarely troubled New Englanders, did ministers lose control in one fell swoop, and it came to be their worst and final embarrassment, as coffeehouse skeptics like Robert Calef clucked over benighted Puritan ideas. Such Yankees had come a long way, and the future belonged to them.

Notes

1. Rutman, American Puritanism, 133.

2. McGiffert, "American Puritan Studies in the
   1960's," 45-46, 42; Perry Miller and Thomas H.
   Johnson, The Puritans (New York, 1938), 1; Miller,
   The New England Mind: The Seventeenth Century,
   vii.

3. Miller, The New England Mind: The Seventeenth
   Century, vii; Dunn, Puritans and Yankees: The
   Winthrop Dynasty of New England, 1630-1717 (Princeton, 1962), vi; Rutman, Winthrop's Boston, 278-
   279; Lucas, Valley of Discord: Church and Society
   Along the Connecticut River, 1636-1725 (Hanover,
   1976), 203-204. As McGiffert has explained,
   reference "to the 'monolithic' structure of
   seventeenth-century New England society and
   thought has been common among historians who
   treat the eighteenth century and find it useful,
   as Miller did, to set the fragmentation of the
   latter period over against the comparative unity
   and simplicity of the former." McGiffert,
   "American Puritan Studies in the 1960's," 41.

4. Mather, Magnalia, III, 128, 65; Selement, "Publication and the Puritan Minister," 226; Hosmer,
   ed., Winthrop's Journal, II, 260.

5. David D. Hall, ed., The Antinomian Controversy,
   1636-1638, A Documentary History (Middletown,
   1968), 212; Emery Battis, Saints and Sectaries:
   Anne Hutchinson and the Antinomian Controversy in
   the Massachusetts Bay Colony (Chapel Hill, 1962),
   129-133; Williston Walker, The Creeds and Platforms
   of Congregationalism (Philadelphia: Pilgrim Press
   edition, 1969), 133-134.

6. Mather, Magnalia, Book III, 65; Samuel Eliot Morison, ed., Of Plymouth Plantation, 1620-1647 (New
   York, 1976), 316, 320.

7. Frederick C. Drake, "Witchcraft in the American
   Colonies, 1647-1662," American Quarterly, XX
   (1968), 698; Burr, ed., Narratives of the Witchcraft Cases, 136, 408-409.

8. James Axtell, The School upon a Hill (New Haven,

1974), 24-26; Mather, Magnalia, Book III, 142-
143; Margery Somers Foster, "Out of Smalle Beginnings . . ." An Economic History of Harvard
College in the Puritan Period (1636 to 1712)
(Cambridge, Mass., 1962), 88-89.

9. Miller, The New England Mind: From Colony to
Province, 325; Dunn, Puritans and Yankees, 17.

10. Mather, Magnalia, Book III, 151. Estimates of
church membership in colonial America vary
greatly; cf. Butler, "Magic," 317, and Bonomi
and Eisenstadt, "Church Adherence," 275.

11. Mather, Magnalia, Book III, 151; Sibley's Harvard
Graduates, I, 500, 288; Thomas Jefferson Werten-
baker, The Puritan Oligarchy: The Founding of
American Civilization (New York, 1947), 208-251;
Edwin Powers, Crime and Punishment in Early
Massachusetts, 1620-1692, A Documentary History
(Boston, 1966), 324.

12. Mather, Ratio, 142; Adams, Eminently Good and
Useful Men, 38; Sibley's Harvard Graduates, I,
367; Mather, Magnalia, Book III, 154-155, IV,
155; Increase Mather, Wo to Drunkards (Cambridge, Mass., 1673), 20; Green, ed., "Diary
of Increase Mather," 359; Thomas, ed., Diary
of Samuel Sewall, I, 10; "A Letter By Rev.
John Higginson To The County Court, 1670,"
Essex Institute, Historical Collections, VIII,
90; Beales, "The Half-Way Covenant and Religious Scrupulosity," 479-480.

13. Drake, "Witchcraft in the American Colonies,"
697-708; Hansen, Witchcraft at Salem, 12-13.

14. Axtell, The School Upon a Hill, 29; Sibley's
Harvard Graduates, I, 499, 501; Green, ed.,
"Diary of Increase Mather," 359, 346; Mather,
Magnalia, Book III, 138.

15. Sibley's Harvard Graduates, I, 146; Justin Winsor,
ed., The Memorial History of Boston (Boston,
1881), IV, 239, 256-257; Mather, Magnalia, Book
III, 187-188.

16. McLoughlin, New England Dissent, I, 79, 285;
Bremer, The Puritan Experiment, 141; Ford, ed.,
Diary of Cotton Mather, I, 209, II, 536; Sibley's

Harvard Graduates, V, 600; White Kennett to Benjamin Colman, March 13, 1716/7, M.H.S., Proceedings, III (1920), 75.

17. Cotton Mather, Vigilantius (Boston, 1706), 25-26; Increase Mather to _____ _____, January 3, 1676, M.H.S., Collections, 4th Ser., VIII, 90; Sibley's Harvard Graduates, IV, 452; Phillips, An Elegy upon the Deaths of those Excellent and Learned Divines the Reverend Nicholas Noyes, A.M., and the Reverend George Curwin (Boston, 1717), 4; William G. McLoughlin and Martha Whiting Davidson, eds., "The Baptist Debate of April 14-15, 1668," M.H.S., Proceedings, LXXVI (1964), 104.

18. Samuel Cooke, Necessarius (New York, 1731), 47; Mather, Ratio, 106; Cotton, A Funeral Sermon Preach'd at Bristol, 31; Ford, ed., Diary of Cotton Mather, II, 146, 199, 240, 336, 50; Fowler and Dow, eds., "Diary of Rev. Joseph Green," 91.

19. Mather, Wo to Drunkards (Boston, 1712), 33; Cooke, Necessarius, 47; Sibley's Harvard Graduates, V, 319; Thomas, ed., Diary of Samuel Sewall, II, 638; Foster, Their Solitary Way, 151, 152; Benjamin Colman, A Sermon at the Lecture in Boston (Boston, 1717), 29.

20. [Mather], The Pure Nazarite (Boston, 1723), 1-2; Green, ed., "Diary of Increase Mather," 365; Ford, ed., Diary of Cotton Mather, II, 221, 242, 698, 229, 160, 235, 283.

21. Mather, Ratio, 143; Sibley's Harvard Graduates, V, 33; Ford, ed., Diary of Cotton Mather, II, 588; Samuel Phillips, Wisdom, an Essential Requiste (Boston, 1759), 25.

22. Ford, ed., Diary of Cotton Mather, II, 80, 226, I, 134, II, 360-361; Sibley's Harvard Graduates, V, 383, IV, 359-360; Winsor, ed., The Memorial History of Boston, II, 251.

23. Ford, ed., Diary of Cotton Mather, II, 531, 538; Emil Oberholzer, Jr., Delinquent Saints, 39-41.

24. Increase Mather to Michael Wigglesworth, March 8, 1679. and March 12, 1679, M.H.S., Collections, 4th Ser., VIII, 94-96; Sibley's Harvard

Graduates, I, 281-282; Morgan, The Puritan
Family, 55-56; Richard Crowder, No Featherbed to
Heaven: A Biography of Michael Wigglesworth,
1631-1705 (East Lansing, 1962), 212-220.

25. Axtell, The School Upon a Hill, 32; Levin, ed.,
    Bonifacius, 74; Foxcroft, Elisha Lamenting after
    the God of Elijah, 62; Ford, ed., Diary of Cot-
    ton Mather, II, 81, 755, 201, 271; Sibley's
    Harvard Graduates, III, 163; Brown, Divine Help
    Implored, 30; Youngs, God's Messengers, 48-49;
    Mather, Magnalia, "A General Introduction,"
    para. 5.

26. Ford, ed., Diary of Cotton Mather, II, 472, 534,
    348, 225; Turell, The Life and Character of the
    Reverend Benjamin Colman, D.D., 71.

27. Werking, "'Reformation Is Our Only Preservation'
    Cotton Mather and Salem Witchcraft," William and
    Mary Quarterly, 3d Ser., XXIX (1972), 290, 288;
    James Fitch to Increase Mather, July 1, 1684;
    "Samuel Willard's Account of the Strange Case of
    Elizabeth Knapp of Groton," M.H.S., Collections,
    4th Ser., VIII, 475, 559, 558, 562; Burr, ed.,
    Narratives of the Witchcraft Cases, 101, 99, 103,
    129, 122, 124.

28. Sibley's Harvard Graduates, II, 321-322; Charles
    W. Upham, Salem Witchcraft (New York, 1867), II,
    218; Burr, ed., Narratives of the Witchcraft
    Cases, 259, 276.

29. Konig, Law and Society in Puritan Massachusetts:
    Essex County, 1629-1692 (Chapel Hill, 1979),
    169-170; Burr, ed., Narratives of the Witchcraft
    Cases, 321, 349-351, 237.

30. On Hale, Parris and Noyes see Sibley's Harvard
    Graduates, I, 514-517; II, 241-242; Marion L.
    Starkey, The Devil in Massachusetts: A Modern
    Enquiry into the Salem Witch Trials (New York:
    Anchor Book edition, 1969), 44, 211-212, 251;
    Hansen, Witchcraft at Salem, 42-43, 55, 64-65,
    104-105, 148-149, 212-215; Burr, ed., Narratives
    of the Witchcraft Cases, 369-397.

31. Sibley's Harvard Graduates, I, 376-377; Boyer
    and Nissenbaum, Salem Possessed, 9-10, 18-20;
    Murdock, Increase Mather, 294; Starkey, The

<u>Devil in Massachusetts</u>, 191-192; Ford, ed., <u>Diary of Cotton Mather</u>, I, 216.

32. Richard P. Gildrie, <u>Salem, Massachusetts, 1626-1683, A Covenant Community</u> (Charlottesville, 1975), preface; Boyer and Nissenbaum, <u>Salem Possessed</u>, 86-92; <u>Sibley's Harvard Graduates</u>, IV, 293; Bushman, <u>From Puritan to Yankee: Character and the Social Order in Connecticut, 1690-1765</u> (Cambridge, Mass., 1967), preface.

Until recently, historians have simply ignored
the pastoral work of the Puritan clergy, probably
deeming it too mundane to reveal anything relevant to
historiographical issues. Investigating clerical life
in the eighteenth-century, however, Bill Youngs broke
from this perspective and consequently found that
pastoral activities played a key role in the professional life of provincial ministers, especially after
the Great Awakening. Building on David D. Hall's The
Faithful Shepherd (1972), Youngs concluded that the
New England ministry must have progressed through
three distinct stages between 1620 and 1750: "In the
earliest period, the ministers were the admired religious leaders of a relatively harmonious society.
In the second stage, the ministers sought to establish a quasi-aristocratic control over a society of
contending factions. In the third stage, they based
their leadership on the principle of consent." In
each phase, according to Youngs, preachers relied on
a different aspect of their profession to control
parishioners: first the deferred-to-authority, then
the professional expert, and finally the pastoral
shepherd. Of course, Youngs recognized, these
approaches "were, in varying degrees, present among the
clergy throughout the colonial period, but historical
circumstances caused them to emphasize different
parts of their work at different times."[1]

Though Youngs's model meshes well with others
and indeed sprang from a careful reading of Miller,
Hall, and Richard L. Bushman's From Puritan to Yankee
(1967), it does not fit the facts of seventeenth-
century pastoralism. From the founding of New England,
ministers catechized children, led the lost to grace,
battled witches, counseled families, kept peace between neighbors, tended the sick, and aided the poor.
To be sure, it seems like Cotton Mather did more pastoral work than Thomas Shepard, but that impression
comes from the bias of the sources. Mather consis-
tently recorded his pastoral activities; Shepard
rarely did. A careful search of extant records, however, yields enough clues to establish that first-
generation ministers were an earthy lot and close to
their people. To cite one final example, when John
Wilson accompanied soldiers in the Pequot War, they
spotted a warrior "carrying away an English Maid . . .
fearing to kill the Maid if they shot at the Indian,"

the troops asked Wilson's counsel. "God will direct the Bullet," Wilson assured them, and they "shot accordingly; and killed the Indian . . . and saved the Maid." Wilson, then, was neither a cloistered scholar--an elite deferred-to-authority--nor was he a professional expert. Wilson was out among his people, taking risks, giving them seat-of-the-pants advice, and thereby expecting to remain their faithful shepherd. There simply is no evidence, and certainly no quantifiable data, to establish that any one generation excelled in pastoral work. It was always the mainstay of the Puritan ministry.[2]

Nor did the Great Awakening, as almost all historians have argued, introduce evangelism to New England's religious leadership. Far from tribal, the Puritan clergy labored individually with the unchurched to convert them: in their homes, on the streets, aboard ships, and anywhere else they spotted a prospect. "Visit, visit, visit,--more frequently, more fruitfully" was Cotton Mather's motto. And his intention during such "Savoury Conferences" was, like that of Peter Thacher of Milton, to make New Englanders' "Hearts burn within them" or, like Noyes of Newbury, to rescue the "Entangled out of the Briars." Consequently, pastors contacted and influenced people of all classes and persuasions--whether sailors or governors; poor or rich, red, white, or black; or Jew, Baptist, or skeptic. Indeed, the Great Awakening was a natural, although spectacular, expression of over a century of Puritan evangelism.[3]

This portrayal of Puritan divine as pastor and evangelist is further confirmed by the clergy's writing and distribution of books. Rather than writing for an intellectual community, ministers published mostly sermons to "be Preached a Second Time in the way of the Press." Then they handed them to laymen, believing "in this way you may speak more than you have time to speak in any personal interview." Given that 78% of these works were sermonic and many others, like catechisms, eulogies, and polemical tracts, were similar in purpose, it is a conservative estimate to posit that 90% of the clergy's writings were either pastoral to edify churchgoers or evangelical to proselytize those outside the tribe. Moreover, by circulating such "plain" literature, ministers strove in every generation to fashion and perpetuate a collective mentality in New England. "By good books," concluded Cotton Mather, "there is a salt of piety scattered about a neighborhood."[4]

All such pastoral work and evangelical outreach guaranteed a degree of continuity in New England's history, as ministers personally guarded the people of the region from new social, political, economic, and ideological forces that eventually changed Puritans to Yankees. Their efforts were most successful in witchcraft cases, because three generations of ministers rescued victims and cleared the innocent by using prayer and instruction. "Prayer and Faith," as Cotton Mather summed up a long tradition, "was the Thing which drove the Divils from the Children" of John Goodwin. Not until 1692, when the people turned to legal authorities to "rebuke Satan," did the clergy lose their jurisdiction in matters preternatural. Though they recovered and had the final word about Salem witchcraft, overall the episode secularized New Englanders more by raising doubts about witchcraft lore and the ministerial perpetrators of it. Miller rightly concluded: "The onus of error lay heavy upon the land; realization of it slowly but irresistibly ate into the New England conscience."[5]

Faithful shepherds were far less successful in rescuing New Englanders from worldliness, the lure of "Madame Bubble's" wealth, sensual pleasure, and sophistication. As the region's colonies grew to provinces, the number of unchurched people steadily increased, ever multiplying "profane Swearing and Cursing, evident Sabbath-breaking, Drunkenness, Fighting, Fornication and all Scandalous Unchastities, Cheating, Stealing, an Abandonment unto Idleness, Lying, unrighteous Defamations." Though a "Son of Thunder," the Puritan divine only inhibited these tides of change. Even among the churched by the 1660's emerged a "great & generall neglect of instructing" children in the New England Way. Again, ministers tried to plug the gap by catechizing youngsters and promoting godly education in schools, but these very efforts, while a link to the Puritan past, were also a manifestation and promotion of Yankee culture.[6]

Their greatest failing, however, involved dissenters. Based on the quantity of cases pastors handled, it is clear New England culture became pluralistic before it was either worldly or disillusioned about witchcraft. Possibly this occurred because New England was so religious--so Puritan.

Prosperous merchants and hard-working farmers probably
did feel guilty about neglecting Christian duties or
doubting orthodoxy; and when reminded of God's ways,
they reformed a bit or at least kept quiet. But
Baptists, Quakers, and a host of other innovators
battled Puritans on their own terms, claiming to be
more Protestant or Biblical or Spirit-led than the
Puritans. Thus, when a Puritan or a Yankee turned
dissenter, he did not feel guilty but self-assured,
and whatever tact--sermonic or pastoral--a Puritan
divine employed, the dissenter had this edge.

These dynamics are apparent in the case of Anne
Eaton, wife of Theophilus Eaton, the governor of New
Haven. In 1644, Anne began stalking out of the church
whenever John Davenport performed the rite of infant
baptism or absenting herself from public worship en-
tirely. A mystified Davenport and some of the brethren spoke with Anne, discovering that a book by one
A. R. had led her to reject the Puritan belief that
"baptism had come in the room of circumscision and
therefore might lawfully be administered unto in-
fants." After scrutinizing A. R.'s tract, Davenport
preached two sermons to prove that infant baptism was
Biblical. But Anne remained unconvinced. Davenport
then wrote an item-by-item refutation of A. R.'s
treatise, arranged for Anne's husband "to join with
himself Mr. Gregson and Mr. Hooke to whom probably
she would give ear sooner than to other," and had one
of them read A. R.'s arguments and another then read
Davenport's answers. After two such sessions, William
Hooke, who was Davenport's colleague, and Thomas Gregson, one of the magistrates of New Haven, left both
A. R.'s book and Davenport's rebuttal with Anne for
further study. Her "contemptuous carriage," however,
presaged little hope that all "the pains and patience"
of Davenport and Hooke would bear fruit. Eaton was
fully convinced she was the true Puritan, and even
one modern commentator is "content to apply the term
'Puritan'" to such dissenters.[7]

Continuity and change, therefore, characterized
New England and its ministry. While this is a truism
recognized by every scholar in the field, it has
nonetheless been the habit of historians to emphasize
one or the other, as in Miller's consensus Puritanism
and Rutman's pluralistic Boston. Likewise, Bushman
described Connecticut before 1690 as a "close-knit,
tightly controlled, homogeneous community," while
Lucas found it to be a "valley of discord." Even

historians like Dunn, who wrote of a more gradual
metamorphosis, periodized the Puritan to Yankee process by generations, each wave bringing a new world.
Viewing New England society through the pastoral work
of the clergy, however, reveals that all such models,
if applied rigidly across-the-board, are suspect.
Though dissenters and worldly persons interjected
chaos from the beginning, New Englanders also shared
certain fundamental beliefs that lasted nearly a century. And while it is convenient and somewhat accurate to describe change in neat generational blocks,
it did not always proceed that way. Ministers and
parishioners changed within their own lifetimes in
certain areas, like church polity, and several generations changed little, if at all, on matters such
as witchcraft. Moreover, generations overlapped in
a boggling mix of complexity. Cotton Mather, for
example, cooperated with his father, Increase, to
perpetuate the "true Reformed Religion" of first-
generation ministers, while joining forces with
fourth-generation preachers, like Colman, and even
Baptist preachers, to usher in the new "Catholic
Spirit" of Yankee America. From the pastoral labors
of the Puritan clergy, then, it is clear that each
force for change--dissenters, worldly people, and
new philosophies--and each force for continuity--
sermonic theology, folklore, tradition, and law--
must be analyzed individually and then assigned its
proper setting in the historical mosaic. The historian, as much as any Puritan divine, must be a
"skillful and faithful Vine-Dresser" in his vineyard.[8]

Notes

1. Youngs, God's Messengers, 138.

2. Mather, Magnalia, Book III, 47.

3. Ford, ed., Diary of Cotton Mather, II, 352;
   Mather, The Comfortable Chambers, 25; Mather,
   Magnalia, Book III, 148.

4. Mather, Utilia, iv; Levin, ed., Bonifacius, 77;
   Selement, "Publication and the Puritan Minister,"
   226-227; Murdock, Literature & Theology in Colonial New England, 181.

5. Burr, ed., Narratives of the Witchcraft Cases,
   126, 414; Miller, The New England Mind: From
   Colony to Province, 208.

6. Boyer and Nissenbaum, Salem Possessed, 213;
   Mather, Ratio, 143; Cotton, A Funeral Sermon
   Preach'd at Bristol, 31; Axtell, The School Upon
   a Hill, 29.

7. Newman Smyth, ed., "Mrs. Eaton's Trial (in 1644):
   As It Appears upon the Records of the First
   Church of New Haven," New Haven Colony Histori-
   cal Society, Papers, V (1894), 134-138; Alan
   Simpson, Puritanism in Old and New England
   (Chicago, 1955), 1.

8. Bushman, From Puritan to Yankee, preface; Lucas,
   Valley of Discord, 203-206; Mather, Magnalia,
   "An Attestation"; Ford, ed., Diary of Cotton
   Mather, II, 536; Cooke, Necessarius, 46.

BIBLIOGRAPHY OF WORKS CITED

I. Diaries

Adams, William. "Memoir of the Rev. William Adams."
    Massachusetts Historical Society, Collections,
    4th Series, I (1852), 8-22.

Bumstead, Jeremiah. "Diary of Jeremiah Bumstead of
    Boston, 1722-1727." Edited by S. F. Haven.
    New England Historical and Genealogical Regis-
    ter, XV (1861), 194-315.

Dexter, Samuel. "Extracts from the Diary of Rev.
    Samuel Dexter, of Dedham." New England His-
    torical and Genealogical Register, XIII (1859),
    305-310, XIV (1860), 35-40, 107-112, 202-205.

Green, Joseph. "Diary of Rev. Joseph Green, of Salem
    Village." Edited by Samuel P. Fowler and George
    Francis Dow. Essex Institute, Historical Col-
    lections, VIII (1866), 216-224, X (1869), 73-
    104, XXXVI (1900), 325-330.

Homes, William. "Diary of Rev. William Homes of
    Chilmark, Martha's Vineyard, 1689-1746."
    Edited by Charles E. Banks. New England His-
    torical and Genealogical Register, XLVIII
    (1894), 446-453, XLIX (1895), 413-416, L
    (1896), 155-166.

Mather, Cotton. Diary of Cotton Mather. Edited by
    Worthington Chauncey Ford. New York, 1957.

Mather, Increase. "Diary of Increase Mather."
    Edited by Samuel A. Green. Massachusetts His-
    torical Society, Proceedings, 2nd Series, XIII
    (1899-1900), 340-374, 398-411.

Parkman, Ebenezer. The Diary of Ebenezer Parkman.
    Edited by Francis G. Walett. Worcester, 1974.

Saffin, John. John Saffin His Book (1665-1708).
    Edited by Caroline Hazard. New York, 1928.

Sewall, Samuel. The Diary of Samuel Sewall, 1674-
    1729. Edited by M. Halsey Thomas. New York,
    1973.

Shepard, Thomas. God's Plot: The Paradoxes of Puri-
tan Piety, Being the Autobiography & Journal of
Thomas Shepard. Edited by Michael McGiffert.
Amherst, 1972.

Thacher, Peter. "Thacher's Journal." Edited by
A. K. Teele in his The History of Milton, Mass.,
1640-1887. Boston, 1887. See Appendix B,
6410657.

Wigglesworth, Michael. The Diary of Michael Wiggles-
worth, 1653-1657; The Conscience of a Puritan.
Edited by Edmund S. Morgan. New York: Harper
Torchbooks edition, 1965.

  II. Early New England Histories, Biographies,
         Eulogies & Autobiographies

Bradford, William. Of Plymouth Plantation, 1620-1647.
Edited by Samuel Eliot Morison. New York, 1976.

Chauncy, Charles. "A Sketch of Eminent Men in New
England." Massachusetts Historical Society,
Collections, X (1890), 154-170.

Hutchinson, Thomas. The History of the Colony and
Province of Massachusetts-Bay. 3 vols. New
York: Kraus Reprint, 1970.

Johnson, Edward. Johnson's Wonder-Working Providence,
1628-1651. Edited by J. Franklin Jameson. New
York: Barnes & Noble edition, 1937.

Mather, Cotton. Just Commemorations. Boston, 1715.

_____. Magnalia Christi Americana. London,
1702.

_____. Pillars of Salt. Boston, 1699.

Mather, Increase. "The Autobiography of Increase
Mather." Edited by M. G. Hall. American
Antiquarian Society, Proceedings, LXXI (1961),
271-360.

_____. The Life and Death of the Reverend Man
of God, Mr. Richard Mather. Cambridge, Mass.,
1670.

Mather, Samuel. The Life of the Very Reverend and
    Learned Cotton Mather. Boston, 1729.

Moody, Samuel. A Summary Account of the Life and
    Death of Joseph Quasson. Boston, 1726.

Phillips, Samuel. An Elegy upon the Deaths of those
    Excellent and Learned Divines the Reverend
    Nicholas Noyes, A.M., and the Reverend George
    Curwin. Boston, 1717.

Prince, Thomas. Some Account of those English Minis-
    ters who have successfully presided over the
    Work of Gospelizing the "Indians" on "Martha's
    Vineyard," and the Adjacent Islands. Appended
    to Experience Mayhew, Indian Converts. London,
    1727.

Turell, Ebenezer. The Life and Character of the
    Reverend Benjamin Colman, D.D. Boston, 1749.

Winthrop, John. Winthrop's Journal: History of New
    England, 1630-1649. Edited by James Kendall
    Hosmer. 2 vols. New York: Barnes & Noble edi-
    tion, 1946.

_____. A Short Story of the Rise, reign, and
    ruine of the Antinomians, Familists & Libertines.
    In David D. Hall, ed., The Antinomian Controversy,
    1636-1638: A Documentary History. Middletown,
    Conn., 1968.

III. Funeral Sermons

Adams, Eliphalet. Eminently Good and Useful Men. New
    London, 1720.

Appleton, Nathaniel. The Servant's Actual Readiness
    for the Coming of the Lord, Described, and
    Recommended. Boston, 1752.

Brown, John. Divine Help Implored. Boston, 1726.

Callendar, John. A Discourse Occasioned by the Death
    of the Reverend Mr. Nathaniel Clap. Newport,
    1746.

Colman, Benjamin. The Prophet's Death Lamented. Bos-
    ton, 1723.

Cooke, Samuel. _Necessarius_. New York, 1731.

Cotton, John. _A Funeral Sermon Preach'd at Bristol_. Boston, 1729.

Foxcroft, Thomas. _Elisha Lamenting after the God of Elijah_. Boston, 1737.

Loring, Israel. _Ministers Must Certainly and Shortly Die_. Boston, 1731.

Mather, Cotton. _A Faithful Man, Described and Rewarded_. Boston, 1705.

_____. _The Comfortable Chambers_. Boston, 1728.

Prince, Thomas. _The Departure of Elijah Lamented_. Boston, 1728.

Sewall, Joseph. _When the Godly Cease and the Faithful Fail_. Boston, 1737.

_____. _The Duty, Character and Reward of Christ's Faithful Servants_. Boston, 1758.

Swift, John. _A Funeral Discourse Delivered at Marlborough_. Boston, 1731.

White, John. _The Gospel Treasure in Earthen Vessels_. Boston, 1725.

IV. Treatises

Adams, Hugh. "A Narrative of Remarkable-Instances of a Particular-Faith, And Answers of Prayer." Massachusetts Historical Society Ms.

Bellingham, Richard. _A Copy of the Last Will and Testament of Richard Bellingham, Esqu_. Boston, 1706.

Calef, Robert. _More Wonders of the Invisible World_. In George Lincoln Burr, ed., _Narratives of the Witchcraft Cases_. New York: Barnes & Noble edition, 1946.

Colman, Benjamin. _A Dissertation on the Image of God_. Boston, 1736.

Colman, Benjamin. A Sermon at the Lecture in Boston. Boston, 1717.

Foxcroft, Thomas. Lessons of Caution. Boston, 1733.

Gibbs, Henry. Bethany: Or, The House of Mourning. Boston, 1714.

_____. Godly Children Their Parents Joy. Boston, 1727.

Hale, John. A Modest Enquiry Into the Nature of Witchcraft. In George Lincoln Burr, ed., Narratives of the Witchcraft Cases. New York: Barnes & Noble edition, 1946.

Lawson, Deodat. A Brief and True Narrative. In George Lincoln Burr, ed., Narratives of the Witchcraft Cases. New York: Barnes & Noble edition, 1946.

Mather, Cotton. The Angel of Bethesda. Edited by Gordon W. Jones. Barre, Mass., 1972.

_____. Bonifacius. Edited by David Levin. Cambridge, Mass., 1966.

_____. The Cure of Sorrow. Boston, 1709.

_____. India Christiana. Boston, 1721.

_____. Memorable Providences. In George Lincoln Burr, ed., Narratives of the Witchcraft Cases. New York: Barnes & Noble edition, 1946.

_____. The Pure Nazarite. Boston, 1723.

_____. Ratio Disciplinae Fratrum Nov-Anglorum. Boston, 1726.

_____. Tremenda. Boston, 1721.

_____. Utilia. Boston, 1716.

_____. Vigilantius. Boston, 1706.

_____. Wholesome Words. Boston, 1713.

_____. The Wonders of the Invisible World. In George Lincoln Burr, ed., Narratives of the

Witchcraft Cases. New York: Barnes & Noble edition, 1946.

Mather, Increase. A Brief Discourse. Cambridge, Mass., 1686.

_____. A Dying Legacy of a Minister to His Dearly Beloved People. Boston, 1722.

_____. An Essay for the Recording of Illustrious Providences. Boston, 1684.

_____. Several Sermons. Boston, 1715.

_____. Wo to Drunkards. Cambridge, Mass., 1673, and Boston, 1712.

Mayhew, Experience. Grace Defended, In a Modest Plea for an Important Truth. Boston, 1744.

_____. Indian Converts. London, 1727.

Moody, Samuel. The Doleful State of the Damned. Boston, 1710.

Norton, John. The Orthodox Evangelist. London, 1654.

Odlin, John. Doing Righteousness. Boston, 1742.

Phillips, Samuel. Wisdom, an Essential Requisite. Boston, 1759.

Rawson, Grindal, and Danforth, Samuel. "Account of an Indian Visitation, A.D. 1698." Massachusetts Historical Society, Collections, 1st Series, X, 129-134.

Shepard, Thomas. The Works of Thomas Shepard. Edited by John A. Albro. 3 vols. Boston, 1853.

Wadsworth, Benjamin. The Bonds of Baptism. Boston, 1717.

_____. A Guide for the Doubting. Boston, 1711.

Webb, John. The Greatness of Sin. Boston, 1734.

Williams, William. The Duty of Parents. Boston, 1721.

V.   Letters

Colman, Benjamin.   "Bishop Kennett to Benjamin Colman,"
    Massachusetts Historical Society, Proceedings,
    III (1920), 67-84.

Brattle, Thomas.   "Letter of Thomas Brattle, F. R. S.,
    1692."   In Goerge Lincoln Burr, ed., Narratives
    of the Witchcraft Cases.   New York: Barnes &
    Noble edition, 1946.

Dunton, John.   "John Dunton's Letters from New-En-
    gland."   Prince Society, Publications, IV
    (1867).   Also a Burt Franklin reprint: New
    York, n.d.

Higginson, John.   "A Letter by Rev. John Higginson to
    the County Court, 1670."   Essex Institute, His-
    torical Collections, VIII, 89-90.

"The Mather Papers."   Massachusetts Historical Society,
    Collections, 4th Series, VIII.

VI.   Church Records

Cambridge, Mass.   Thomas Shepard's "Confessions".
    Edited by George Selement and Bruce C. Woolley.
    Colonial Society of Massachusetts, Collections,
    LVIII (1981).

New Haven, Connecticut.   "Mrs. Eaton's Trial (in
    1644); As It Appears upon the Records of the
    First Church of New Haven."   Edited by Newman
    Smyth.   New Haven Colony Historical Society,
    Papers, V (1894), 133-148.

Salem, Mass.   The Records of the First Church in
    Salem Massachusetts 1629-1736.   Edited by
    Richard D. Pierce.   Salem, 1974.

Wenham, Mass. and Chelmsford, Mass.   The Notebook of
    the Reverend John Fiske, 1644-1675.   Edited by
    Robert G. Pope.   Colonial Society of Massachu-
    setts, Collections, XLVII (1974).

VII.   Secondary Sources

Adams, James Truslow.   The Founding of New England.
    Boston, 1921.

Axtell, James. The School upon a Hill: Education and Society in Colonial New England. New Haven, 1974.

Battis, Emery. Saints and Sectaries: Anne Hutchinson and the Antinomian Controversy in the Massachusetts Bay Colony. Chapel Hill, 1962.

Beales, Ross W. "The Half-Way Covenant and Religious Scrupulosity: The First Church of Dorchester, Massachusetts, as a Test Case," William and Mary Quarterly, 3d Series, XXXI (1974), 465-480.

Beinfield, Malcolm Sydney. "The Early New England Doctor: an Adaptation to a Provincial Environment," Yale Journal of Biology and Medicine, XV (1942), 99-132, 271-288.

Benz, Ernst. "Pietist and Puritan Sources of Early Protestant World Missions (Cotton Mather and A. H. Francke)." Church History, XX (1951), 28-55.

Bonomi, Patricia V., and Eisenstadt, Peter R. "Church Adherence in the Eighteenth-Century British Colonies." William and Mary Quarterly, 3d Series, XXXIX (1982), 245-286.

Boorstin, Daniel J. The Americans: The Colonial Experience. New York, 1958.

Boyer, Paul, and Nissenbaum, Stephen. Salem Possessed: The Social Origins of Witchcraft. Cambridge, Mass., 1974.

Bremer, Francis J. The Puritan Experiment: New England Society from Bradford to Edwards. New York, 1976.

Bushman, Richard L. From Puritan to Yankee: Character and the Social Order in Connecticut, 1690-1765. Cambridge, Mass., 1967.

Butler, Jon. "Magic, Astrology, and the Early American Religious Heritage, 1600-1760." American Historical Review, LXXXIV (1979), 317-346.

Child, Frank Samuel. The Colonial Parson of New England: A Picture. New York, 1896.

Crowder, Richard. No Featherbed to Heaven: A Biography of Michael Wigglesworth, 1631-1705. East Lansing, 1692.

Demos, John. "Underlying Themes in the Witchcraft of Seventeenth-Century New England." American Historical Review, LXXV (1970), 1311-1326.

Drake, Frederick C. "Witchcraft in the American Colonies, 1647-1662." American Quarterly, XX (1968), 694-725.

Dunn, Richard S. Puritans and Yankees: The Winthrop Dynasty of New England, 1639-1717. Princeton, 1962.

Eggleston, Edward. The Transit of Civilization: From England to America in the Seventeenth Century. Boston: Beacon edition, 1959.

Foster, Margery Somers. "Out of Smalle Beginnings..." An Economic History of Harvard College in the Puritan Period (1636 to 1712). Cambridge, Mass., 1962.

Foster, Stephen. Their Solitary Way: The Puritan Social Ethic in the First Century of Settlement in New England. New Haven, 1971.

Gay, Peter. A Loss of Mastery: Puritan Historians in Colonial America. Berkeley, 1966.

Geddes, Gordon E. Welcome Joy: Death in Puritan New England. Ann Arbor, 1981.

Gildrie, Richard P. Salem, Massachusetts, 1626-1683, A Covenant Community. Charlottesville, 1975.

Green, Lorenzo Johnson. The Negro in Colonial New England, 1620-1776. New York, 1942.

Greven, Philip J., Jr. "Historical Demography and Colonial America," William and Mary Quarterly, 3d Series, XXIV (1967), 438-454.

Hall, David D. The Faithful Shepherd: A History of the New England Ministry in the Seventeenth Century. Chapel Hill, 1972.

Hall, David D. "The World of Print and Collective
    Mentality in Seventeenth-Century New England."
    In John Higham and Paul K. Conkin, eds., New
    Directions in American Intellectual History.
    Baltimore, 1979.

Hansen, Chadwick. Witchcraft at Salem. New York,
    1969.

Holmes, Thomas James. Increase Mather: A Bibliog-
    raphy of His Works. 2 vols. Cleveland, Ohio,
    1931.

Jones, James W. The Shattered Synthesis: New England
    Puritanism Before the Great Awakening. New
    Haven, 1973.

Kellaway, William. The New England Company, 1649-
    1776, Missionary Society to the American Indians.
    London, 1961.

Kittredge, George Lyman. Witchcraft in Old and New
    England. Cambridge, Mass., 1929.

Konig, David Thomas. Law and Society in Puritan
    Massachusetts: Essex County, 1629-1692.
    Chapel Hill, 1979.

Leach, Douglas Edward. The Northern Colonial Fron-
    tier, 1607-1763. New York, 1966.

_____. Flintlock and Tomahawk: New England in
    King Philip's War. New York, 1958.

Levy, Babette May. "Early Puritanism in the Southern
    and Island Colonies," American Antiquarian
    Society, Proceedings, LXX (1960), 67-348.

Lockridge, Kenneth A. Literacy in Colonial New En-
    gland: An Enquiry into the Social Context of
    Literacy in the Early Modern West. New York,
    1974.

Lovelace, Richard F. The American Pietism of Cotton
    Mather: Origins of American Evangelicalism.
    Grand Rapids, 1979.

Lucas, Paul R. Valley of Discord: Church and Society
    Along the Connecticut River, 1636-1725. Hanover,
    New Hampshire, 1976.

McGiffert, Michael. "American Puritan Studies in the 1960's." William and Mary Quarterly, 3d Series, XXVII (1970), 36-67.

McLoughlin, William G. New England Dissent, 1630-1833, The Baptists and the Separation of Church and State. 2 vols. Cambridge, Mass., 1971.

McLoughlin, William G., and Davidson, Martha Whiting, eds. "Introduction." In "The Baptist Debate of April 14-15, 1668." Massachusetts Historical Society, Proceedings, LXXVI (1964), 91-104.

Miller, Perry. Errand Into the Wilderness. New York: Harper Torchbooks edition, 1964.

_____ The New England Mind: the Seventeenth Century. New York, 1939.

_____. The New England Mind: From Colony to Province. Cambridge, Mass., 1953.

_____, and Johnson, Thomas J. The Puritans. New York, 1938.

Moran, Gerald F. "Religious Renewal, Puritan Tribalism, and the Family in Seventeenth-Century Milford, Connecticut." William and Mary Quarterly, 3d Series, XXXVI (1979), 236-254.

Moran, Gerald F., and Vinorskis, Manis A. "The Puritan Family and Religion: A Critical Reappraisal." William and Mary Quarterly, 3d Series, XXXIX (1982), 29-63.

Morgan, Edmund S. "The Historians of Early New England." In Ray Allen Billington, ed., The Reinterpretation of Early American History: Essays in Honor of John Edwin Pomfret. New York: Norton edition, 1968.

_____. The Puritan Family: Religion & Domestic Relations in Seventeenth-Century New England. New York: Harper Torchbooks edition, 1966.

_____. "The Puritans and Sex." New England Quarterly, XV (1942), 591-607.

Morison, Samuel Eliot. Builders of the Bay Colony. Boston: Sentry edition, 1958.

Morison, Samuel Eliot. Harvard College in the Seventeenth Century. 2 vols. Cambridge, Mass., 1936.

Murdock, Kenneth Ballard. Increase Mather: The Foremost American Puritan. Cambridge, Mass., 1926.

_____. "Introduction." In his Selections from Cotton Mather. New York: Hafner edition, 1960.

_____. Literature & Theology in Colonial New England. Cambridge, Mass., 1949.

Oberholzer, Emil, Jr. Delinquent Saints: Disciplinary Action in the Early Congregational Churches of Massachusetts. New York, 1956.

Pope, Robert G. The Half-Way Covenant: Church Membership in Puritan New England. Princeton, 1969.

_____. "New England Versus the New England Mind: The Myth of Declension." Journal of Social History, III (1969-1970), 301-318.

Powers, Edwin. Crime and Punishment in Early Massachusetts: 1620-1692, A Documentary History. Boston, 1966.

Ronda, James P. "'We Are As Well As We Are': An Indian Critique of Seventeenth-Century Christian Missions." William and Mary Quarterly, 3d Series, XXIV (1977), 66-82.

Rutman, Darrett B. "God's Bridge Falling Down: 'Another Approach' to New England Puritanism Assayed." William and Mary Quarterly, 3d Series, XIX (1962), 408-421.

_____. "The Mirror of Puritan Authority." In Michael McGiffert, ed., Puritanism and the American Experience. Reading, Mass., 1969.

_____. Winthrop's Boston: A Portrait of a Puritan Town, 1630-1649. Chapel Hill, 1965.

Selement, George. "Publication and the Puritan Divine." William and Mary Quarterly, 3d Series, XXXVII (1980), 219-241.

Selement, George. "Perry Miller: A Note on His Sources in The New England Mind: The Seventeenth Century." William and Mary Quarterly, 3d Series, XXXI (1974), 453-464.

_____. "The Meeting of Elite and Popular Minds at Cambridge, New England, 1638-1645." William and Mary Quarterly, 3d Series, forthcoming 1984.

Shipton, Clifford K. "A Plea for Puritanism." American Historical Review, XL (1935), 460-467.

Sibley, John Langdon, and Shipton, Clifford K. Sibley's Harvard Graduates: Biographical Sketches of Those Who Attended Harvard College. Cambridge, Mass., 1873-1975.

Simpson, Alan. Puritanism in Old and New England. Chicago, 1955.

Skotheim, Robert Allen. "The Writing of American Histories of Ideas: Two Traditions in the XXth Century." Journal of the History of Ideas, XXV (1964), 257-278.

Slotkin, Richard. "Narratives of Negro Crime in New England, 1675-1800." American Quarterly, XXV (1973), 3-31.

Stannard, David E. "Death and Dying in Puritan New England." American Historical Review, LXXVIII (1973), 1305-1330.

_____. The Puritan Way of Death: A Study in Religion, Culture, and Social Change. New York, 1977.

Starkey, Marion L. The Devil in Massachusetts: A Modern Enquiry into the Salem Witch Trials. Anchor Books edition, 1969.

Thomas, Keith. Religion and the Decline of Magic. New York, 1971.

Upham, Charles W. Salem Witchcraft. New York, 1867.

Vaughan, Alden T. New England Frontier: Pruitans and Indians, 1620-1675. Boston, 1965.

Walker, Williston. The Creeds and Platforms of Con-
     gregationalism. Philadelphia: Pilgrim Press
     edition, 1960.

Weis, Frederick Lewis. The Colonial Clergy and the
     Colonial Churches of New England. Lancaster,
     Mass., 1936.

Werking, Richard H. "'Reformation Is Our Only Pre-
     servation'" Cotton Mather and Salem Witchcraft."
     William and Mary Quarterly, 3d Series, XXIX
     (1972), 281-290.

Wertenbaker, Thomas Jefferson. The Puritan Oligarchy:
     The Founding of American Civilization. New York,
     1947.

Winslow, Ola Elizabeth. Meetinghouse Hill 1630-1783.
     New York, 1952.

Winsor, Justin, ed. The Memorial History of Boston.
     4 vols. Boston, 1881.

Youngs, J. William T., Jr. God's Messengers: Reli-
     gious Leadership in Colonial New England, 1700-
     1750. Baltimore, 1976.

_____. "Perry Miller and the 'Buzzing Facuality'
     of Colonial New England." Paper read before the
     meeting of the American Historical Association,
     Washington, D.C., December 29, 1980.

DATE DUE
